CREATION V. EVOLUTION:

WHAT THEY WON'T TELL YOU IN BIOLOGY CLASS

What Christians Should Know About Biblical Creation

Daniel A. Biddle, Ph.D. (editor)

E-mail: dan@genesisapologetics.com

Genesis Apologetics, Inc.
P.O. Box 1326
Folsom, CA 95763-1326

CREATION V. EVOLUTION:
What They Won't Tell You in Biology Class
What Christians Should Know About Biblical Creation
by Daniel A. Biddle, Ph.D. (editor)

Printed in the United States of America

ISBN 9781628717761

www.xulonpress.com

Dedication

To my wife, Jenny, who supports me in this work. To my children Makaela, Alyssa, Matthew, and Amanda, and to your children and your children's children for a hundred generations—this book is for all of you. To Dave Bisbee and Mark Johnston, who planted the seeds and the passion for this work. To Cole Thompson and Jake Bienvenue who guided the topics selected for this work, may you continually grow in your faith. To Leigh Bashor, whose fine review and polish refined this work. Thank you all!

"Guard what has been entrusted to you, avoiding worldly and empty chatter and the opposing arguments of what is falsely called "knowledge"—which some have professed and thus gone astray from the faith. Grace be with you."—1 Tim. 6:20–21

"This is the Lord's doing; it is marvelous in our eyes." — Psalm 118:23

Contents

About the Authors

David V. Bassett, M.S. earned his Bachelor of Science in Geology at the University of Texas in El Paso and a Master's of Science in Geological Science from Columbia Pacific University, maintaining a 4.0 post-graduate academic record. He is a high school science teacher with over 28 years experience in Christian education and has been the Science Department Head of Ovilla Christian School in Ovilla, TX since March 1996. Since then, he has been at the Creation Evidence Museum, located on the bank of the Paluxy River in Glen Rose, Texas, where he has served as the Assistant to the Director, Dr. Carl E. Baugh. Mr. Bassett is a voting member of the Creation Research Society and is the current president of the Metroplex Institute of Origin Science for the Dallas-Ft. Worth area.

Dr. Jerry Bergman has five Master's degrees in the science, health, psychology, and biology fields, a Ph.D. in human biology from Columbia Pacific University, and a Ph.D. in measurement and evaluation from Wayne State University. Jerry has taught biology, genetics, chemistry, biochemistry, anthropology, geology, and microbiology at Northwest State Community College in Archbold OH for over 27 years. He is currently an Adjunct Associate Professor at the University of Toledo Medical School. He has over 900 publications in 12 languages and 32 books and monographs, including

Vestigial Organs Are Fully Functional. He has also taught at the Medical College of Ohio as a research associate in the department of experimental pathology, at the University of Toledo, and at Bowling Green State University. Jerry is also a member of MENSA, a Fellow of the American Scientific Association, a member of The National Association for the Advancement of Science, and member of many other professional associations. He is listed in Who's Who in America, Who's Who in the Midwest and in Who's Who in Science and Religion.

Dr. Daniel A. Biddle has a Ph.D. in Organizational Psychology from Alliant University in San Francisco, California, an M.A. in Organizational Psychology from Alliant, and a B.S. in Organizational Behavior from the University of San Francisco. Daniel is the CEO of Biddle Consulting Group, Inc. in Folsom, California, a Human Resources consulting practice. Daniel's specialty area includes statistical analysis, research methodologies, and Equal Employment Opportunity consulting. Daniel has worked as an expert consultant and/or witness in over 80 state and federal cases. Daniel's ministry experience includes over two decades of Church service and completing graduate work at Western Seminary.

Roger Patterson is a writer and editor with Answers in Genesis, one of the largest Creation Ministries in the U.S. Roger earned his B.S. Ed. degree in biology and chemistry from Montana State University-Billings. Before joining Answers in Genesis, he taught high school students for eight years in Wyoming's public school system and assisted the Wyoming Department of Education in developing assessments and standards for use in its schools. For many years, he taught from an evolutionary perspective in his classroom until God opened his eyes to the truth of Scripture.

Dr. Jonathan D. Sarfati has a B.Sc. (Hons.) in Chemistry and a Ph.D. in Spectroscopy (Physical Chemistry). Dr. Sarfati is a research scientist and editorial consultant for Creation Ministries International (CMI) in Brisbane. In this capacity, he is co-editor of Creation magazine, and also writes and reviews articles for *Journal of Creation*, CMI's in-depth, peer-reviewed publication, as well as contributing to CMI's website, http://www.creation.com. Dr. Sarfati has authored or co-authored several notable books, including *Refuting Evolution* (now over 500,000 copies in print), *The Creation Answers Book*, *Refuting Evolution 2*, *Refuting Compromise*, *15 Reasons to Take Genesis as History*, *By Design: Evidence for Nature's Intelligent Designer—the God of the Bible*, and *The Greatest Hoax on Earth? Refuting Dawkins on Evolution*.

Roger Sigler, M.A. is a licensed professional geoscientist in the State of Texas. His diverse background in geology spans oil and gas exploration, core analysis, geothermal systems, groundwater problems, and environmental abatement projects. His latest employment is in core, geological, and drilling fluid analyses at Intertek's Westport Technology Center. He is also a part-time geology instructor at Wharton County Junior College. He has taught creation science since 1989, and helped form the Greater Houston Creation Association where he was president from 1997-2001. He acquired a Master's degree in Geology from the Institute for Creation Research in 1998. He has been published in the 1998 and 2003 *Proceedings of the International Conference on Creationism* and co-authored a poster session on catastrophic debris flows at the 2011 Geological Society of America. He is a member of the Geological Society of America, Houston Geological Society, American Association of Petroleum Geologists, and Creation Research Society. He is married, has two children, and attends Christ Covenant Church in Houston, Texas.

Dr. Jeff Tomkins has a Ph.D. in Genetics from Clemson University, a M.S. from the University of Idaho, and a B.S. from Washington State University. He was on the Faculty in the Department of Genetics and Biochemistry, Clemson University, for a decade, where he published 57 secular research papers in peer-reviewed scientific journals and seven book chapters on genetics, genomics, proteomics, and physiology. For the past several years, Dr. Tomkins has been a Research Scientist at the Institute for Creation Research and an independent investigator publishing ten peer-reviewed creation science journal papers, numerous semi-technical articles, and two books including *The Design and Complexity of the Cell*.

Dr. Jay L. Wile holds an earned Ph.D. in nuclear chemistry and a B.S. in chemistry, both from the University of Rochester. He has been awarded more than $200,000 in research grants from the National Science Foundation, and his award-wining research has produced 30 articles in the peer-reviewed scientific literature. He has taught at both the university and high school levels, but he is best known for his very popular "*Exploring Creation With*" series of science textbooks.

Cornelius Van Wingerden, M.S. taught high school science and math for 21 years. He retired from teaching high school in 2011. Van holds a B.S. in Geology from San Diego State University, an M.S. in Geology from the ICR Graduate School, Santee, California, and a M.A. in Science Education from California State University, Bakersfield. While at ICR, he studied large debris flows found in the Kingston Peak Formation, Death Valley Region.

Preface

Daniel A. Biddle, Ph.D.

This book is essential for any high school or college-aged Christian attending public school—especially before taking biology and earth science classes. Most biology and earth science classes in today's public schools teach evolutionary theory as fact, and only rarely mention creation possibilities outside of this theory, such as Biblical Creation.

Did you know that **44%** of young adults who abandon their Christian faith started developing their doubts in high school?[1] When these "ex-Christians" are asked, "What makes you question the Bible the most," **40%** gave responses that had to do with Biblical Creation, including Noah's Flood, the age of the Earth, and the Genesis account. This book, written by leading Creation Scientists, provides solid answers to these critical questions that will help Christian high school and college students solidify their faith to withstand the evolution-based teaching that is so prevalent in today's schools.

The evolutionary teaching included in most public school biology and earth science classes starkly contrasts the Biblical Creation account. In some cases, when not taught *both* creation and evolution perspectives, young Christians lose their faith, or end up with a watered-down faith that robs them of the abundant life that Christ longs to provide.

Today, Christians hold different beliefs about origins. Sometimes these differences can lead to wide and tense divisions within the Church. This book was not written to widen the existing divide. While one's position on origins is critical when it comes to holding to the authority of Scripture, love and acceptance between brothers and sisters in the faith are also important. Indeed, without maintaining relationships with each other, these dialogues regarding origins cannot even take place.

With this said, this book is written from a "Young Earth" origins position for three reasons. First, I believe that this is the most obvious and plain interpretation of Scripture. That is, God conveyed his Word to us in a way that the six-day creation story would be understood as written, such as in Genesis 1 and Exodus 20:11. Secondly, after reviewing the creation evidence, I believe the science stacks heavily in the "young" direction. Finally, with biblical teachers being held to a higher level of accountability (James 3:1), I find it assuring to convey the creation account given in the Bible using the *original and obvious* language the Lord provided.

According to a recent Gallup poll, when over 1,000 Americans[2] are surveyed about human beginnings and creation, 46% respond by affirming a "young" Earth that is less than 10,000 years old. This percentage has remained almost constant, averaging about 45% from 1982 to today. Alternative views included "theistic evolution" (the belief that humans evolved under God's guidance) with 32% of the responses, and secular evolution at 15%.[3] Looking at this more broadly, "some 78% of Americans today believe that God had a hand in the development of humans in some way, just slightly less than the percentage who felt this way 30 years ago."

I am saddened by so many people going through life not knowing about their Creator or His Creation in ways that He intended for us all to know through His Word. So many people live and die without knowing and experiencing three important truths: (1) God created *one human race in general* (Genesis 1), (2) each of us are created *specifically* by God ("For you created my inmost being; you knit me together in my mother's womb," Psalm 139:13), and (3) we are each created with *intention and purpose for this life* ("And we know that in all things God works for the good of those who love him, who have been called according to his purpose," Romans 8:28).

Personally, I find it very reassuring to see *and* experience a union between God's Word and His Creation. It's amazing to just take walks in the mountains and see how massive rock and sediment layers were curled up and buckled by Noah's *cataclysmic* Flood when the continental plates were shifted as God destroyed the "old world" (2 Peter 3:6). Clearly, an earth-shattering process occurred when God "blotted out *every living thing* that was upon the face of the land, from man to animals to creeping things and to birds of the sky, and they were blotted out from the earth" (Genesis 7:23). At times, God even gives hints about the process that was involved in such a re-creation of the face of the world:

> He established the earth upon its foundations, so that it will not totter forever and ever. You covered it with the deep as with a garment; the waters were standing above the mountains. At Your rebuke they fled. At the sound of Your thunder they hurried away. *The mountains rose; the valleys sank down to the place which You established for them*. You set a boundary that they may not pass over, So that they will not return to cover the earth. (Psalms 104:5–9, NASB)

The topics included in this book were selected by reviewing the evolutionary topics covered in most high school and college biology and earth science textbooks, then surveying Christian students on the topics that seemed to be most convincing. There are many other important topics that could be included in a book like this, but we let the students choose (by survey) which ones were most important to them. What follows are mostly scientific reasons why the most convincing evolutionary arguments have not convinced us, and thus why we believe the Bible had it right all along.

Overview of the Book

The Introduction of the book provides a discussion regarding the importance of the perspectives that we bring to understanding our origins, including the assumptions required and faith required for both the evolutionary and creationist positions. It also discusses the importance of the topics covered by this book, and how they can shape our worldviews which can permeate virtually every part of our lives.

The first two chapters don't (directly) have much to do with biology or earth sciences, but they are provided to explore the foundation of the Christian faith, including the reliability and inspiration of the Bible and Noah's Flood. These two chapters are provided first to provide a background of the Christian faith before investigation of the scientific evidence that supports it.

Chapter 1 answers the question "Can We Trust the Bible?" by looking at the "big picture" of the Bible (i.e., how it was assembled) while also focusing on one particular chapter of the Bible (Isaiah 53) because of its significance to Christians. It also contains evidence that became available to test the Bible's reliability after the Dead Sea Scrolls were discovered.

Chapter 2 covers Noah's Flood and provides compelling evidence from around the world that the Flood really did happen—exactly as described in the Bible. The evidence reviewed includes a review of the major fossil deposits around the world, coal deposits, Earth's sedimentary rocks, how the Flood was involved in shaping the mountains and landscapes, and some specifics regarding the feasibility of Noah's Ark, such as its dimensions and how all of the various animals could have fit.

Chapter 3 reviews some of the challenges and inaccuracies of the common methods that are used to date the age of the Earth in an effort to prove evolution. Additional evidences which provide clues to a younger creation are also reviewed, including coal deposits, diamonds, soft tissues that are supposedly millions of years old, and the ocean. This chapter is important because mainstream biology textbooks will even admit that an "ancient world" is essential for supporting evolutionary theory: "Evolution takes a long time. If life has evolved, then Earth must be very old...Geologists now use radioactivity to establish the age of certain rocks and fossils. This kind of data could have shown that the Earth is young. If that had happened, *Darwin's ideas would have been refuted and abandoned.* Instead, radioactive dating indicates that Earth is about 4.5 billion years old—plenty of time for evolution and natural selection to take place"[4] (emphasis added).

Chapters 4 and 5 deal with the fossil record. Chapter 4 investigates the fossil record, including "ancestral," "transitional," and "divergent" forms that are necessary for the theory of evolution and "gradualism" to hold up. Chapter 5 reviews the fossil findings that are commonly held up by evolutionists as proof that man evolved from earlier forms of ape-like creatures, including several of the well-known examples such as "Lucy."

Chapter 6 reviews fundamental evolution teachings, such as natural selection and evolution. This chapter answers difficult questions such as "Do Darwin's Finches Prove Evolution?" Chapter 7 takes a careful look into one of the "poster children" of evolution theory: Whale evolution.

Chapter 8 looks into the differences and similarities between human and chimp DNA. This chapter is divided into "basic," "intermediate," and "advanced" discussions of this topic.

Chapter 9 discusses "vestigial structures" (such as the human appendix), which are supposedly parts of our bodies that are "leftovers" from the evolutionary process and are therefore "no longer necessary." This chapter reveals that each and every part of our bodies are engineered by God with purpose and intention. Helpful resources and websites are provided at the end of the book.

Introduction

Roger Patterson

Have you ever heard the phrase "the facts speak for themselves"? Well, stop and think about it for a moment. Is it true? The answer is no. Sure, there might be some facts that when put together can seem to have only one explanation, but that is not always the case.

Every fact must be *interpreted* to really have any meaning. Think about a fossil, for instance. We could make a list of observations, facts, about the fossil. We could record its mass, measure various dimensions, describe the type of minerals it is made of, etc. Those are observations—data everyone can agree on. We could measure its density using different methods and ask somebody to repeat our tests so that they could verify our results.

But what about questions like: "How old is the fossil?" or "How did the creature die?" The fossil doesn't have a tag attached to it with answers to those questions. The fossil—the fact—cannot speak for itself to tell us those answers. In order to come to conclusions, the facts must be interpreted. Because people interpret evidence, they will naturally be biased in the way they think. No matter what anyone tells you, they do have some bias. The basic set of biases you have is called your worldview. We use our worldview like a set of glasses to help us see the world clearly.

As we think about scientific study, we really need to think about it in two categories. First, there is operational or observational science. This is the type of scientific study that the scientific method helps us do. We observe, test, and repeat experiments to try to obtain a consistent result. We can create lots of great technologies by applying observational science. For instance, since chemical reactions are predictable, we know that when certain chemicals mix together, we will get a certain reaction. This has allowed us to make airbags, medicines, fuels, and all kinds of useful things.

Second, there is historical science, also referred to as origins or forensic science. This is when we take the things we know about the present (from observational science) and try to figure out the past. For example, if I find a fossil fish in a layer of rocks, I can make all kinds of observations, but to answer how the fish got in the rock layer, how it died, or how long ago that happened, I have to interpret those observations. I put the pieces together with other things I know and try to understand the history of this fish.

Which type of science do you think is more accurate and reliable, observational or historical? Well, determining the age of the fish fossil (historical science) requires a lot more interpretation and relies on more assumptions than measuring the bones or doing a chemical analysis to see what minerals are in the rock that surround it (observational science). We must be much more careful with the conclusions of historical science because worldview influences historical science much more than observational science.

What We Believe Really Matters

If I told you that I know a man who walked on water, would you believe me? The way you answer that question is going to reveal some of your bias. Someone might reply that they know the density of a person is greater than the density of water, so the person would sink if they tried to walk on water. We would call this person an empiricist—they demand experimental evidence to believe something—at least, that's what they say about themselves. Another might respond that it is against the laws of nature—this person might be a materialist or a naturalist, insisting that miracles can't happen.

But what about Jesus? Didn't He walk on water? Sure He did. Did I see Him? No. Was it normal? No. But I believe He walked on water because I look at the world from a Christian worldview, or a biblical worldview. Similarly, I believe God created the entire universe just as the Bible describes, not from a big bang billions of years ago. I believe He created the different kinds of plants and animals and that they did not evolve over millions of years. I have faith that all of these things are true, but it is not a blind faith. My faith is based on something bigger than myself. It is "the substance of things hoped for, the evidence of things not seen" (Hebrews 11:1).

Many will say that this viewpoint makes my thinking unscientific. I disagree. That is only true if I accept that scientists must deny the existence of miracles and rely entirely on a materialistic or naturalistic worldview. In other words, the materialist who believes that the universe only consists of matter and energy has *faith* that is the case! After all, he can't always detect spiritual truths with his broken ways of thinking (2 Corinthians 4:4). The empiricist has to exercise faith that his senses are reliable because there is no way to test his senses without using his senses. These people are putting their faith in themselves and their own thinking. They have faith that the universe created itself from nothing; I have faith that God created the universe from nothing.

Everyone puts their faith in something. Rather than a blind faith, I choose to put my faith in Jesus Christ, the Creator and Sustainer of the universe (Hebrews 1:1–4). Knowing that He created everything and having a written record of the history of the universe in the Bible, I have a great starting point to begin thinking about the world around me. When I think about science, I am trying to understand how God made things and how He designed them to work and live together with other organisms.

The God of Science

God must exist for science to even be possible! When a scientist performs an experiment, he expects nature to behave according to the laws it has shown in the past. When was the last time you put a teapot on the stove and expected it to freeze? Why does the world follow these laws? Because all known laws arise from lawgivers, the only rational answer is that there was a Lawgiver—the God of the Bible—who created the universe to follow certain patterns we call laws. In fact He tells us that we should expect nature to behave in a uniform way; for example, in Genesis 8:22. But that doesn't mean that He can't intervene at times in miraculous ways, as we see described in the Bible.

Logic is another necessity for scientific study. But what is logic? You can't smell it, take its temperature, or see what color it is. It is immaterial (not made of matter) and is true everywhere in the universe. How can a materialistic worldview account for something that is not made of matter? It can't. Logic is only rational if God exists and has created the universe and our human minds in a special way. Similar to chemical or physical laws, the laws of logic upon which every thought rests also require a Lawgiver. The Bible tells us that God thinks, and He has created mankind in His image. We are able to use our God-given reason to understand the world around us.

So, if God did not exist, there would be no consistent laws of nature and no logic. We wouldn't be able to understand the world around us. Science is impossible without the Creator God of the Bible. Now, there are a lot of fancy philosophical arguments that people try to use to get away from the truth that God exists, but these people are using the very brains that God gave them to try to tell you He doesn't exist. The Apostle Paul helps us to understand why this is so in Romans 1:18–32 and 1 Corinthians 1:18–31. If the universe came from a random event like the big bang and everything formed thereafter by random chance, why would we expect to find order, laws of logic, and laws of nature? Why would we expect to find anything at all? We wouldn't. So to say that God cannot be a part of our science and history is not rational.

Absolute Authority

How do you know what is true? Do people get to vote on truth? Can truth change over time? These are important things to consider as we study science and try to understand things in the present and the past. As we consider claims made by textbooks, teachers, or video documentaries, many of the ideas are going to be contrary to Scripture. Many of the arguments may appear to be convincing and there may be lots of evidence used to support the claims, but what if these ideas are different than the Bible's claims? Which authority, God's Word or man's words, are you going to trust? There are only two choices! We can either look to a human authority—man determines truth—or a biblical standard—God determines truth.

For example, scientists who embrace evolutionary interpretations of genetics claim that there was never a single couple at the beginning of the human race. Rather, they claim there was a larger population of original humans. If we accept that, then we have to reject God's description of specially creating Adam and Eve as the first pair that gave rise to every human on the Earth (Genesis 1–4). We even must then reject Jesus' references to the first couple, for example in Mark 10:6! Likewise, you would have to reject that there was ever a Tower of Babel from which all of the different people groups emerged. If you start from the wrong starting point you always come to the wrong conclusions.

The Bible contains a true, eyewitness testimony (God Himself) of the creation of the world. If we build our thinking about science and history and every other subject from God's Word, we have a true foundation to build upon. If we build our thinking on man's ideas apart from the Bible, we are starting from a subjective position invented by God-rejecting sinners rather than a true position. You must decide who you are going to trust.

Two Revelations

God has revealed Himself to man in two ways—*general* and *special* revelation. God has created a universe for us to study and learn about Him. Psalm 19 tells us that the heavens declare the glory of God. Romans 1 tells us that mankind can know certain things about God by looking at the creation. The design that is obvious in nature points to the Designer. All of this is referred to as God's general revelation given to everyone through all of time.

God has given man the task of studying His creation and using that knowledge to rule over the Earth and its creatures (Genesis 1:26–28). But this general revelation is limited. For example, what could you learn about God from a virus killing a dog or a tiger killing a deer to eat it? What about all of the terrible diseases in the world? What do they teach us about God?

To answer these questions rightly, we must look to special revelation—the Bible. God has revealed many wonderful truths in the Bible that we would not know otherwise. Many people doubt that God is good because of all of the evil in the world. But the Bible tells us that the world was not always like this—it is broken. God created the world in a perfect state about 6,000+ years ago. He created all of the animals and man to be vegetarians (Genesis 1:29–31). Adam's disobedience and sin broke the world (the Fall of man) and brought a curse from God (Genesis 3) that will someday be lifted (Romans 8:20–22). The Father sent His Son to redeem man from his sin, and one day, the Son will come again and the world will be restored to its original perfection—no more disease or death, forever.

The Bible is not a textbook that tells us about the structure of atoms or the way the digestive system works. But without the special revelation given to us as a starting point, we cannot rightly understand the general revelation we see in the world around us. Where the Bible does speak to scientific issues, we know we can trust it.

Table 1 provides several examples that demonstrate this. Scientists through the centuries have often erred in matters of science. But not the Holy Bible, which has been shown to be scientifically accurate. While the Bible is not primarily a science text, many scientific matters are mentioned in passing; and when mentioned, with careful study they can be confirmed to be accurate![5]

Table 1. The Bible and Science Agree

Formerly Believed	**Currently Believed**	**The Bible Always Said**
Only between one thousand and twelve hundred stars in the whole universe.	Trillions upon trillions of stars; they cannot be counted by man!	Jeremiah 33:22a "As the host of heaven ***cannot be numbered***..."
The Earth is flat.	The Earth is round.	Isaiah 40:22a "It is he that sits upon the ***circle*** of the earth..."

Light does not move, it is just there.	Light moves and has physical properties; "light waves" or photons.	Job 38:19a "Where is the way where ***light dwells***? ..."
The Steady State Theory, the stars are just out there.	Each star is unique, and two of the star constellations have gravitational binding.	Job 38:31 "Can you bind the sweet influences of **Pleiades**, or loose the bands of **Orion**?"
Bad blood should be bled out, to make a person well.	Blood is vital to life, sometimes a transfusion is needed to add blood.	Leviticus 17:11a "For the ***life of the flesh is in the blood***:..."
Air has no weight, it is just there.	Oxygen, nitrogen, carbon-dioxide have respective atomic weights that can be measured.	Job 28:25a "To make the ***weight for the winds***..."
Winds blow straight across the Earth.	Air currents move in large circular patterns.	Ecclesiastes 1:6b "... and ***the wind returns again according to his circuits***."
The Earth is carried on someone's back.	The Earth floats free in space.	Job 26:7b "... and ***hangs the earth upon nothing***."
People just get sick; hand washing is not important.	Many diseases spread by contact; wash your hands in running water.	Leviticus 15:13b "... and wash his clothes, and ***bathe his flesh in running water***..."
The stars are all similar to each other.	Each and every star is actually unique.	I Corinthians 15:41b "... for ***one star differs from another star*** in glory."
Something from nothing for no reason – "The Big Bang" model (poof! look a universe!)	Every action has an equal and opposite reaction; that is real science. Cause and effect; input is needed to make output.	Genesis 1:1 "In the beginning God created the heaven and the earth."

Apologetics—Giving a Defense of the Faith

If you are a Christian, you are going to face challenges to your faith from many different angles. The key to withstanding these challenges is found from the writings of the Apostle Peter, a man who knew trials:

> But even if you should suffer for righteousness' sake, you are blessed. 'And do not be afraid of their threats, nor be troubled.' But sanctify the Lord God in your hearts, and always be ready to give a defense to everyone who asks you a reason for the hope that is in you, with meekness and fear; having a good conscience, that when they defame you as evildoers, those who revile your good conduct in Christ may be ashamed. For it is better, if it is the will of God, to suffer for doing good than for doing evil. (1 Peter 3:14–17, NKJV)

We get the term apologetics from this verse. The Greek word *apologia* is translated as "reason" or "defense" in this passage. It doesn't mean that we are to apologize, but that we provide an explanation for why we believe what we believe. Just as evangelism is sharing the good news of forgiveness in sins through Jesus, apologetics is sharing the reasons the Bible can be trusted, by giving biblical explanations for scientific models (e.g., how Noah's Flood can explain the rock layers and fossils or how radiometric dating can't be trusted).

So you can see that apologetics and evangelism are very tightly connected. Explaining why we think and believe the Bible is true in its descriptions of historical and scientific ideas should always be connected to why we believe it is true with respect to spiritual things. If the Bible's history can't be trusted, why should we trust what it says about spiritual matters? Since we know God is a God of truth, we can trust the historical, scientific, and spiritual truths He has revealed to us in the Bible.

The key to apologetics is to set apart Christ as Lord in your heart, fully trusting in Jesus for your salvation and as the Creator and revealer of truth. You will never know the answer to every question you are asked, but you can trust that there are reasonable answers from the Bible or from a biblical understanding of the world. There are many people who can help you find answers, other Christians who can support you and encourage you with fellowship and prayer. Getting support from your family and church is another important aspect of standing firm in your faith.

You will likely encounter other Christians who believe they can accept the big bang or evolution and still trust the Bible. That is simply not possible, since those theories directly contradict the Bible. However, responding to such people in gentleness and respect is essential. Many Christians have not considered the contradiction in the order of events between the Bible and evolutionary ideas, the problem of death before sin, the meaning of a historical Adam, and the global effects of Noah's Flood. Point them to the Bible as the ultimate authority by which we must judge every other idea. Show them how well the facts fit the Scriptures in a way that makes them want to understand.

When we have the opportunity to challenge claims that are contrary to Scripture, we must make sure that we are asking or responding in a gentle and respectful way. We can trust that the Holy Spirit will help us respond in love and truth, always relying on God's Word as our absolute authority. In the end, the study of science and defending our faith must share the hope of eternal life in the Lord Jesus Christ. In other words, debunking evolution or showing the errors in the big bang theory can be helpful, but there is no hope of salvation from sin in scientific theories. We should always practice the skill of telling people about who Jesus is and what He has done to provide salvation to all who believe.

Chapter 1:

Can We Trust the Bible?

Daniel A. Biddle, Ph.D.

Why is this Chapter Important?

Recent research has revealed a serious epidemic with today's Christian youth. So many are caught up in an unfortunate pattern that goes something like this:[6]

1. They grow up in a Christian home and attend church regularly, but they don't receive solid biblical teaching or training regarding various worldviews;
2. Their faith is challenged by evolutionary teaching when they attend public high school or college;
3. Their questions and doubts go unanswered because of their complacency, lack of interest, or the failure of parents and/or church leadership to equip them with biblical grounding and a solid awareness of various worldviews; and
4. They fall away from their faith, and their generational Christian line is lost.

Many teens today are in Step 1 above, some are in Steps 2–3, and some are recovering from Step 4. Fortunately, some have not entered the cycle above because of their biblical grounding. Whatever your current position, we encourage you to *slowly and steadily* take in the words of this book, beginning with this Chapter about the most important book in history—the Bible.

Overview

So many people ask: Who wrote the Bible? How was the Bible put together? How do we know the Bible stories actually happened? How do we know that it has been accurately translated over the years? These are all fair questions. To start answering some of these questions, we will begin by looking at the big picture, then follow with closer look.

The big picture begins with the Bible's 66 books (39 books in the Old Testament and 27 books in the New Testament) which were written by over 40 different authors from various walks of life, including scholars, kings, priests, shepherds, farmers, physicians, tent-makers, fishermen, and philosophers. The first books of the Bible were compiled around 1450 B.C. and the last books before A.D. 90—a timespan of about 1,500 years. It was written in three languages: Hebrew, Aramaic, and Greek. The most important characteristic of the Bible—and one that makes it different than every other book ever published—is that it is inspired by God (2 Timothy 3:16–17 and 2 Peter 1:19–21).

Despite such a diverse background, the Bible is unlike any other book written in history in its historical accuracy, agreement with demonstrable science and archaeology, and consistency—both internally and externally. The Bible has been translated into over 2,000 languages, and ranks highest among the most widely printed and studied books in the world.

Let's take a closer look into how the Bible was put together. The first 39 books of the Bible (the Old Testament) were solidified and used authoritatively in its complete form by the Hebrews well before Christ. The books of the New

Testament were written between about A.D. 30 and A.D. 90 and were formally "canonized" into the set of 27 books we have today sometime before the year A.D. 375 The word "canon" comes from the Greek word "kanon," which means *measuring rod*. This word was used by those who officially verified an assembled set of 27 books because they stood up to the measuring tests of "divine inspiration and authority."

What led to this final "canonization" process? Theology and history books have thousands of pages on this topic. So we'll consider just a few highlights between the time the New Testament was *inspired* by God through original manuscripts men wrote and *assembled* into the "final canon":[7]

- Paul regarded Luke's writings to be as authoritative as the Old Testament (1 Timothy 5:18; see also Deuteronomy 25:4 and Luke 10:7).
- Peter recognized Paul's writings as Scripture (2 Peter 3:15–16).
- Some of the books of the New Testament were being circulated among the churches (Colossians 4:16; 1 Thessalonians 5:27).
- Clement of Rome mentioned at least eight New Testament books (A.D. 95).
- The writings of Ignatius of Antioch acknowledged about seven New Testament books (A.D. 115).
- The writings of Polycarp, a disciple of John the apostle, acknowledged 15 of the books (A.D. 108). Later, Irenaeus mentioned 21 New Testament books (A.D. 185).
- Hippolytus of Rome recognized 22 of them (A.D. 170–235).

Before the final set of 27 books was formally recognized, an earlier "canon" was compiled in A.D. 170. This Canon, called the Muratorian Canon, included all of the

New Testament books except Hebrews, James, and 3 John. These three books were already God-inspired even though the members of the Muratorian Canon may not have recognized them as so. In A.D. 363, the Council of Laodicea stated that only the Old Testament and the 27 books of the New Testament were to be read in the churches. The Council of Hippo (A.D. 393) and the Council of Carthage (A.D. 397) also affirmed the same 27 books as authoritative.

We owe these ancient councilmen. They sifted through false gospels and other writings that early deceivers claimed were God-inspired so that later generations of Christians could trust, study, know, teach and believe in the Scriptures. Some of the features they recognized in the canon were:

- Did the text describe mythological or pointless miracles, or genuine miracles which always accompanied and authorized a message—the Gospel.
- Did the people who lived through the events that the text describes reject those texts as being false, or accept them as having occurred as described?
- Did the text contain any logical or biblical contradictions? If so, it must not have come from the same Divine co-author, Who is not a God of confusion, but of order—and Who is passionate about clearly revealing who He is to as many as will listen; and,
- Was the text written by an apostle or one authorized by an apostle?

After this "canonization" period, a definitive version of the Bible was recorded in Greek, called the *Codex Vaticanus* in about A.D. 350 The classic King James version, as well as the New King James, relied on the very important *Textus Receptus* copies of Scripture. The Codex is one of the oldest extant manuscripts of the Greek Bible (Old and New Testament), and has been kept in the Vatican Library since the 15th century. Another ancient Bible is the *Aleppo Codex*, which is a medieval bound manuscript of the Hebrew Bible written around A.D. 930. The first English translation of the Bible was made in A.D. 1382 by John Wycliffe was the first book ever mass-produced on the printing press in A.D. 1454 by Johannes Gutenberg.[8]

How Do We Know the Bible is Trustworthy?

Given this brief history of the Bible, let's put the Bible through some tests that historians use when analyzing the historical accuracy and reliability of ancient manuscripts. First, let's evaluate whether *what we have today matches what was written originally*. In the Bible's case, this was about 2,000 years ago and earlier. Second: *Do the recorded events describe true events*? Let's see how the Bible holds up to each of these important questions.

Does the Bible We Have Today Match the Original?

One of the primary ways to answer this important question is to look at the *time gap* between the original writing (called the *autograph*) and the copies that still exist today. As a general rule, the closer the copy is to the original, the greater the accuracy and reliability. Ancient manuscripts like the Bible were written on fragile material such as papyrus, which is a thin paper-like material made from papyrus plants. Because papyrus eventually decays or gets worn out, ancient writers would continually make new copies using this material and others.[9]

Dating these ancient texts is done by a variety of methods, such as analyzing the material on which it was written, letter size and form, punctuation, text divisions, ornamentation, the color of the ink, and the texture and color of the parchment.[10]

Table 2 shows the results of this "test of time" for the Biblical New Testament compared to several other historical documents.

Table 2. How the New Testament Compares to Other Ancient Writings[11]

Author/Work	Date Written	Earliest Copies	Time Gap	# Copies
Homer (Iliad)	800 B.C.	400 B.C.	400 yrs.	643
Herodotus (History)	480–425 B.C.	A.D.900	1,350 yrs.	8
Thucydides (History)	460–400 B.C.	A.D.900	1,300 yrs.	8
Plato	400 B.C.	A.D. 900	1,300 yrs.	7
Demosthenes	300 B.C.	A.D. 1100	1,400 yrs.	200
Caesar (Gallic Wars)	100–44 B.C.	A.D. 900	1,000 yrs.	10
Tacitus (Annals)	A.D 100.	A.D. 1100	1,000 yrs.	20
Pliny (Natural)	A.D. 61–113	A.D. 850	750 yrs.	7
Secundus (History)				
New Testament (Fragment)	A.D. 50–100	A.D. 114	50 yrs.	5,366
New Testament (Books)		A.D. 200	100 yrs.	
New Testament (Most Content)		A.D. 250	150 yrs.	
New Testament (Complete)		A.D. 325	225 yrs.	

Table 2 reveals two important facts. First, the New Testament has many more original copies compared to several other famous pieces of literature (5,366 compared to only hundreds for other famous texts). Second, it reveals that the time span between the original and these copies is closer than almost any other work compared!

Answering the important question, "*Is the Bible we have today what was written down originally*?" is to evaluate the *number of manuscript copies* that were made of the original. Generally speaking, the greater number of copies of the original available, the easier it is to reproduce the original. Taking the 5,366 copies of the New Testament and adding the copies from other languages (such as Latin, Ethiopic, and Slavic) results in more than 25,000 total manuscripts (hand-written copies) that pre-date the printing press in the 15th century! By comparison, the runner-up historical text (Homer's Iliad) has only 643.[12]

With this, the New Testament clearly passes both the *time gap* and the *number of manuscript copies* tests. And if the New Testament doesn't pass this test, one must certainly disregard most other historical texts as inaccurate and/or unreliable!

There is more.

Have you ever had a computer crash, resulting in a total loss of all your data? I have—it's definitely not fun! One of the most difficult challenges about computer crashes is losing the *original copies* of your important homework assignments or work reports. However, when I've experienced these situations, I'm usually able to completely reconstruct all of my important "final versions" through my *email files* because I sent copies of the final versions to friends and/or clients. This is the same situation with the original bible documents and the letter exchanges between the Church Fathers—we can completely reconstruct over 99% of the original Bible (New Testament) from just their letters!

Even if all of the copies of the Bible from A.D. 300 to today were destroyed, the complete New Testament (except for only 11 verses)[13] could be reconstructed using only quotations by the Early Church Fathers in the first few hundred years after Christ! This is because the Church Fathers frequently quoted large sections of Scripture in their letters to each other. In addition, if these Church Fathers quoted from the entire New Testament, then the New Testament had to have been widely circulating before this time—long enough to be regarded as reliable by the early church. This shows that the entire New Testament was already assembled and considered reliable within 50 years from the disciples.[14]

Is What Was Written in the Bible True?

Three of the four Gospels, books that include the narrative of Jesus' life, were written by *direct eye witnesses* of the events in Jesus' life: Matthew, Mark, and John. Luke, when writing the story of Jesus' life for Theophilus, a high-ranking official at the time,[15] wrote: "Many have undertaken to draw up an account of the things that have been fulfilled among us, *just as they were handed down to us by those who from the first were eyewitnesses and servants of the word*" (Luke 1:1–2, emphasis added). Luke continues to state that he carefully vetted his account of Jesus' life and ministry: "With this in mind, since I myself have carefully investigated everything from the beginning, I too decided to write an orderly account for you, most excellent Theophilus, so that you may know the certainty of the things you have been taught" (Luke 1:3–4). Additional examples of this careful research and transcription include:

- 1 John 1:3: "We proclaim to you what we have seen and heard, so that you also may have fellowship with us. And our fellowship is with the Father and with his Son, Jesus Christ."

- 2 Peter 1:16: "For we did not follow cleverly devised stories when we told you about the coming of our Lord Jesus Christ in power, but we were eyewitnesses of his majesty."
- John 20:30–31: "Jesus performed many other signs in the presence of his disciples, which are not recorded in this book. But these are written that you may believe that Jesus is the Messiah, the Son of God, and that by believing you may have life in his name."

In addition, several of the writers of the New Testament did their writing and speaking among people who were present at the events of Jesus life. For example, in Acts 2:22, Peter stated while under interrogation, "Fellow Israelites, listen to this: Jesus of Nazareth was a man accredited by God to you by miracles, wonders and signs, which *God did among you through him, as you yourselves know*" (emphasis added). Paul used this reference to his audience's common knowledge of Christ when he defended himself against Festus: "What I am saying is true and reasonable. *The king is familiar with these things*, and I can speak freely to him. I am convinced that none of this has escaped his notice, because it was not done in a corner" (Acts 26:25–26, emphasis added).

Further, most of the writings of the New Testament were written during a time when the community knew about Jesus, Jesus' followers, or knew of people who did, like parents. "For what I received I passed on to you as of first importance: that Christ died for our sins according to the Scriptures, that he was buried, that he was raised on the third day according to the Scriptures, and that he appeared to Cephas, and then to the Twelve. After that, he appeared to more than five hundred of the brothers and sisters at the same time, most of whom are still living, though some have fallen asleep" (1 Corinthians 15:3–6, emphasis added).

Finally, consider the fact that 11 of the 12 disciples died terrible deaths—being killed for their unchanging testimony of who Christ was, and of His resurrection. They were so sure that Christ was who He claimed to be that they signed their testimony with their own blood!

Isaiah 53 and the Dead Sea Scrolls

In 1947, shepherds chasing a lost sheep in the caves above the Qumran Valley northwest of the Dead Sea made one of the most significant archaeological discoveries of our time—the Dead Sea Scrolls. The scrolls were found in numerous clay jars, and numbered over 900, 200 of which include numerous sections and fragments of every book in the Old Testament except the book of Esther. Though few of its scholars dare admit it, they even contain fragments of several New Testament books.[16]

One of the most significant scrolls is called the "Great Isaiah Scroll," which includes the same Book of Isaiah that we have today in modern bibles, but dates to 125 B.C.[17] The Great Isaiah Scroll is significant for two reasons. First, it was written before the Lord Jesus Christ was yet born and it includes a chapter (Chapter 53) which includes specific and clear prophecies about the torture, death, burial, and resurrection of Christ. Second, its discovery now allows us to test three versions of the Bible representing different time periods: Pre-Christ Dead Sea Scroll, A.D. 930, and today. We can even compare how the English translation of this important text survived or changed through the years!

Table 3 provides a word-by-word comparison of these three versions so you can see for yourself how reliable the translation process has been through the millennia:

Table 3. Comparison of Isaiah 53 between the Dead Sea Scrolls, the Aleppo Codex, and the Modern Bible [18]

Verse	Dead Sea "Great Isaiah" Scroll (125 B.C.)	Aleppo Codex (A.D. 930)	Modern Translation (NIV)
1	Who has believed our report and the arm of YHWH [(1)] to whom has it been revealed?	Who would have believed our report? And to whom hath the arm of the LORD been revealed?	Who has believed our message and to whom has the arm of the LORD been revealed?
2	And he shall come up like a suckling before us and as a root from dry ground there is no form to him and no beauty to him and in his being seen and there is no appearance that we should desire him.	For he shot up right forth as a sapling, and as a root out of a dry ground; he had no form nor comeliness that we should look upon him, nor beauty that we should delight in him.	He grew up before him like a tender shoot, and like a root out of dry ground. He had no beauty or majesty to attract us to him, nothing in his appearance that we should desire him.
3	He is despised and rejected of men, a man of sorrows and knowing grief and as though hiding faces from him he was despised and we did not esteem him.	He was despised, and forsaken of men, a man of pains, and acquainted with disease, and as one from whom men hide their face: he was despised, and we esteemed him not.	He was despised and rejected by men, a man of sorrows, and familiar with suffering. Like one from whom men hide their faces he was despised, and we esteemed him not.
4	Surely our griefs he is bearing and our sorrows he carried them and we esteemed him beaten and struck by God and afflicted.	Surely our diseases he did bear, and our pains he carried; whereas we did esteem him stricken, smitten of God, and afflicted.	Surely he took up our infirmities and carried our sorrows, yet we considered him stricken by God, smitten by him, and afflicted.

5	and he is wounded for our transgressions, and crushed for our iniquities, the correction of our peace was upon him and by his wounds he has healed us.(2)	But he was wounded because of our transgressions, he was crushed because of our iniquities: the chastisement of our welfare was upon him, and with his stripes we were healed.	But he was pierced for our transgressions, he was crushed for our iniquities; the punishment that brought us peace was upon him, and by his wounds we are healed.
6	All of us like sheep have wandered each man to his own way we have turned and YHWH has caused to light on him the iniquity of all of us.	All we like sheep did go astray, we turned every one to his own way; and the LORD hath made to light on him the iniquity of us all.	We all, like sheep, have gone astray, each of us has turned to his own way; and the LORD has laid on him the iniquity of us all.
7	He was oppressed and he was afflicted and he did not open his mouth, as a lamb to the slaughter he is brought and as a ewe before her shearers is made dumb he did not open his mouth.	He was oppressed, though he humbled himself and opened not his mouth; as a lamb that is led to the slaughter, and as a sheep that before her shearers is dumb; yea, he opened not his mouth.	He was oppressed and afflicted, yet he did not open his mouth; he was led like a lamb to the slaughter, and as a sheep before her shearers is silent, so he did not open his mouth.
8	From prison and from judgment he was taken and his generation who shall discuss it because he was cut off from the land of the living. Because from the transgressions of his people a wound was to him	By oppression and judgment he was taken away, and with his generation who did reason? for he was cut off out of the land of the living, for the transgression of my people to whom the stroke was due.	By oppression and judgment he was taken away. And who can speak of his descendants? For he was cut off from the land of the living; for the transgression of my people he was stricken.
9	And they gave wicked ones to be his grave and (3) rich ones in his death although he worked no violence neither deceit in his mouth.	And they made his grave with the wicked, and with the rich his tomb; although he had done no violence, neither was any deceit in his mouth.	He was assigned a grave with the wicked, and with the rich in his death, though he had done no violence, nor was any deceit in his mouth.

10	And YHWH was pleased to crush him and He has caused him grief. If you will appoint his soul a sin offering he will see his seed and he will lengthen his days and the pleasure of YHWH in his hand will advance.	Yet it pleased the LORD to crush him by disease; to see if his soul would offer itself in restitution, that he might see his seed, prolong his days, and that the purpose of the LORD might prosper by his hand:	Yet it was the LORD's will to crush him and cause him to suffer, and though the LORD makes his life a guilt offering, he will see his offspring and prolong his days, and the will of the LORD will prosper in his hand.
11	Of the toil of his soul he shall see {+light+} and he shall be satisfied and by his knowledge shall he make righteous even my righteous servant for many and their iniquities he will bear.	Of the travail of his soul he shall see to the full, even My servant, who by his knowledge did justify the Righteous One to the many, and their iniquities he did bear.	After the suffering of his soul, he will see the light [of life] and be satisfied; by his knowledge my righteous servant will justify many, and he will bear their iniquities.
12	Therefore I will apportion to him among the great ones and with the mighty ones he shall divide the spoil because he laid bare to death his soul and with the transgressors he was numbered, and he, the sins of many, he bore, and for their transgressions he entreated.	Therefore will I divide him a portion among the great, and he shall divide the spoil with the mighty; because he bared his soul unto death, and was numbered with the transgressors; yet he bore the sin of many, and made intercession for the transgressors.	Therefore I will give him a portion among the great, and he will divide the spoils with the strong, because he poured out his life unto death, and was numbered with the transgressors. For he bore the sin of many, and made intercession for the transgressors.

Notes: (1) The tetragrammaton (YHWH) is one of the names of the God of Israel used in the Hebrew Bible. (2) There is a scribal thumb print over lines 10 to 12 in the Dead Sea "Isaiah" Scroll (lines 10–12 include verses 5–7 in modern Bibles). However, while this obscures some letters, all letters are "reconstructible with certainty" (see: http://www.ao.net/~fmoeller/qum-44.htm); (3) a scribbled word probably accusative sign "eth."

Reading the three columns in Table 3 shows an incredibly high degree of similarity. In fact, regarding this specific Chapter in Isaiah, renowned Christian philosopher and apologist Norman Geisler writes:

> Of the 166 words in Isaiah 53, there are only 17 letters in question. Ten of these letters are simply a matter of spelling, which does not affect the sense. Four more letters are minor stylistic changes, such as conjunctions. The remaining three letters comprise the word "light" which is added in verse 11, and does not affect the meaning greatly. Furthermore, this word is supported by the Septuagint and IQ Is [first cave of Qumran, Isaiah scroll]. Thus, in one chapter of 166 words, there is only one word (three letters) in question after a thousand years of transmission—and this word does not significantly change the meaning of the passage.[19]

How is this possible? How can these three different documents, being translated and transcribed over a 2,000 year timeframe, with such *exact* similarity? One explanation is simply that God watched over the process. Practically speaking, he used many incredible scribes to do it. For example, the Talmudists (Hebrew scribes and scholars between A.D. 100 and A.D. 500) had an incredibly rigorous system for transcribing biblical scrolls. Samuel Davidson describes some of the disciplines of the Talmudists in regard to the Scriptures:[20]

> A synagogue roll must be written on the skins of clean animals, prepared for the particular use of the synagogue by a Jew. These must be fastened together with strings taken from clean animals. Every skin must contain a certain number of columns, equal throughout the entire codex. The length of each column must not extend over less than 48 or more than 60 lines; And the breadth must consist of thirty letters. The whole copy must be first-lined; And if three words be written without a line, it is worthless. The ink should be black, neither red, green, nor any

> other color, and be prepared according to a definite recipe. An authentic copy must be the exemplar, from which the transcriber ought not in the least deviate. No word or letter, not even a yod, must be written from memory, the scribe not having looked at the codex before him... Between every consonant the space of a hair or thread must intervene; Between every new parashah, or section, the breadth of nine consonants; Between every book, three lines. The fifth book of Moses must terminate exactly with a line; But the rest need not do so. Besides this, the copyist must sit in full Jewish dress, wash his whole body, not begin to write the name of God with a pen newly dipped in ink, and should a king address him while writing that name, he must take no notice of him.

Why is Isaiah 53 so important to Christians? Because Isaiah 53 includes at least 12 highly specific prophecies regarding the life, death, and resurrection of Christ. The details in this chapter would not be nearly as important if they were written after Christ's birth, but the fact that we can confirm that the chapter was in fact written before Christ proves beyond reasonable doubt both the accuracy and Divine authorship of the Bible. Consider these 12 prophecies, written by Isaiah about 700 years before Christ was even born, alongside references of their New Testament fulfilments:

1. He would not be widely believed (John 1:10–12).
2. He would not have the look of Majesty (Luke 2:7).
3. He would be despised and suffer (Matthew 26:67–68; 27:39–43).
4. He would be concerned about health needs (Matthew 8:17) and would die for our sins (1 Peter 2:24).
5. His pain/punishment would be for us (Matthew 28:20; Romans 4:25).

6. All of us have sinned (Romans 3:10–18).
7. He would not respond to charges (Matthew 26:63).
8. He was to be oppressed and killed (Matthew 26:65–68).
9. He was associated with criminals during life and at death (Matthew 27:38; 27:57–60).
10. He would be buried in a rich man's tomb (Isaiah 53:9).
11. He would be crushed, suffer and die, yet live (Luke 23:44–48; Luke 24:36–44).
12. He would bear our sins (1 Peter 2:24).
13. He would have a portion with the great (Philippians 2:8–11).

The very fact that it has now been confirmed that this was written before Christ is amazing. How could anyone fulfill each of these prophecies, many of which happened after Christ's death and were clearly out of His control (i.e., if he wasn't God)? Finally, consider these prophecies about Christ that were all penned before He was born, and their fulfilments:[21]

Table 4. Forty-three (43) Prophecies Fulfilled by Jesus

Prophecies About Jesus	Old Testament Scripture	New Testament Fulfillment
Messiah would be born in Bethlehem.	Micah 5:2	Matthew 2:1; Luke 2:4–6
Messiah would be born of a virgin.	Isaiah 7:14	Matthew 1:22–23; Luke 1:26–31
Messiah would come from the line of Abraham.	Gen. 12:3; Gen. 22:18	Matthew 1:1; Romans 9:5
Messiah would be a descendant of Isaac.	Gen. 17:19; Gen. 21:12	Luke 3:34
Messiah would be a descendant of Jacob.	Numbers 24:17	Matthew 1:2

Messiah would come from the tribe of Judah.	Genesis 49:10	Luke 3:33; Hebrews 7:14
Messiah would be heir to King David's throne.	2 Sam. 7:12-13; Isa. 9:7	Luke 1:32–33; Romans 1:3
Messiah's throne will be anointed and eternal.	Ps. 45:6-7; Daniel 2:44	Luke 1:33; Hebrews 1:8–12
Messiah would be called Immanuel.	Isaiah 7:14	Matthew 1:23
Messiah would spend a season in Egypt.	Hosea 11:1	Matthew 2:14–15
Children would be massacred at Messiah's birthplace.	Jeremiah 31:15	Matthew 2:16–18
A messenger would prepare the way for Messiah.	Isaiah 40:3-5	Luke 3:3–6
Messiah would be rejected by his own people.	Psalm 69:8; Isaiah 53:3	John 1:11; John 7:5
Messiah would be a prophet.	Deuteronomy 18:15	Acts 3:20–22
Messiah would be preceded by Elijah.	Malachi 4:5-6	Matthew 11:13–14
Messiah would be declared the Son of God.	Psalm 2:7	Matthew 3:16–17
Messiah would be called a Nazarene.	Isaiah 11:1	Matthew 2:23
Messiah would bring light to Galilee.	Isaiah 9:1-2	Matthew 4:13–16
Messiah would speak in parables.	Ps.78:2-4; Isaiah 6:9-10	Matthew 13:10-15,34–35
Messiah would be sent to heal the brokenhearted.	Isaiah 61:1-2	Luke 4:18–19
Messiah would be a priest after Melchizedek order.	Psalm 110:4	Hebrews 5:5–6
Messiah would be called King.	Ps. 2:6; Zechariah 9:9	Matthew 27:37; Mark 11:7–11
Messiah would be praised by little children.	Psalm 8:2	Matthew 21:16
Messiah would be betrayed.	Ps. 41:9; Zech.11:12-13	Luke 22:47–48; Matt. 26:14–16

Messiah's betrayal money used to buy a potter's field.	Zechariah 11:12-13	Matthew 27:9–10
Messiah would be falsely accused.	Psalm 35:11	Mark 14:57–58
Messiah would be silent before his accusers.	Isaiah 53:7	Mark 15:4–5
Messiah would be spat upon and struck.	Isaiah 50:6	Matthew 26:67
Messiah would be hated without cause.	Ps. 35:19; Psalm 69:4	John 15:24–25
Messiah would be crucified with criminals.	Isaiah 53:12	Matthew 27:38; Mark 15:27–28
Messiah would be given vinegar to drink.	Psalm 69:21	Matthew 27:34; John 19:28–30
Messiah's hands and feet would be pierced.	Ps. 22:16; Zech. 12:10	John 20:25–27
Messiah would be mocked and ridiculed.	Psalm 22:7-8	Luke 23:35
Soldiers would gamble for Messiah's garments.	Psalm 22:18	Luke 23:34; Matthew 27:35-36
Messiah's bones would not be broken.	Exodus 12:46; Ps.34:20	John 19:33-36
Messiah would be forsaken by God.	Psalm 22:1	Matthew 27:46
Messiah would pray f or his enemies.	Psalm 109:4	Luke 23:34
Soldiers would pierce Messiah's side.	Zechariah 12:10	John 19:34
Messiah would be buried with the rich.	Isaiah 53:9	Matthew 27:57-60
Messiah would resurrect from the dead.	Ps.16:10; Ps. 49:15	Matthew 28:2-7; Acts 2:22–32
Messiah would ascend to heaven.	Psalm 24:7–10	Mark 16:19; Luke 24:51
Messiah would be seated at God's right hand.	Ps. 68:18; Ps. 110:1	Mark 16:19; Matthew 22:44
Messiah would be a sacrifice for sin.	Isaiah 53:5–12	Romans 5:6-8

Chapter 2:

Did Noah's Flood Really Happen?

Van Wingerden, M.S. & Daniel A. Biddle, Ph.D.

Why is this Chapter Important?

Because the Bible is very specific about Noah's Flood—including the approximate date, the people involved, the nature of the Flood, and the complete worldwide obliteration of all land-dwelling animals—there are only two logical positions to have on the topic: (1) it happened as described in the Bible, or (2) it didn't happen at all. There are no "middle choices." What are the implications for each of these two positions?

If it happened as described in the Bible, we can extract certain lessons that can even apply to our lives today. These include: (1) there is a God who hates sin and judged the entire world for it, (2) the Bible is inspired by God (because the event was foretold and required supernatural power to complete), and (3) God gave the world a massive "do-over" opportunity. There are more, but these are some of the basics that have substantial implications in our lives today. If it didn't happen as described in the Bible, these truths are on unstable ground and the billions of fossils around the world are in need of some other explanation. In this Chapter, we hope to share with the reader some of the key evidence that we have found regarding Noah's Flood that have led us to the first choice: It really happened as described by the Bible.

Overview

Geology text books, especially at the college level, describe many advancing and retreating oceans occurring over millions of years that deposited the sedimentary rocks found on the North American continent. Tens of thousands of feet of sediment are deposited on the continent along with millions of fossils found in the layers. The rock layers found in Grand Canyon of Arizona are given as evidence for the many advancing and retreating oceans. The fossils found in these layers are also used to show the many changing environments taking place during the millions of years while animals were evolving.

This Chapter will refute this conventional theory and present an alternate explanation: the worldwide, catastrophic Flood that happened in the time of Noah. The data, sedimentary structures and fossils, found in the rocks will show that the rock layers deposited in the Grand Canyon and the North American continent did not take millions of years. When you read this chapter, ask yourself what makes more sense while thinking what the truth is.

There is plenty of evidence from various sources in support of a worldwide flood in the past. The scientific evidence actually shows that some kind of flood was destructive and utterly catastrophic. It rearranged the entire Earth's surface. Much of the geography or landscape we see today is a result of that flood. It deposited most of the fossils and sediments we observe today. The flood also involved slamming landmasses that shoved great mountains upward. All over the world we can see evidence of this in common roadside geology (see Figure 1 as an example).

Figure 1. Example of Landmasses that "Buckled" During Noah's Flood

The flood we know from science matched *Noah's Flood,* and was a worldwide, catastrophic event that will never occur again.[22] It completely wiped out all living land animals except those on board Noah's Ark. There is much observable evidence for Noah's Flood in the rock record, historical accounts, and the Bible. In this chapter, we will investigate some of these.

The Fossil Record

Most people are fascinated with fossils; especially big fossils like dinosaurs, or small ones like birds, reptiles and fish that are well preserved and not broken apart. But many people are unaware that finding a whole fossil intact with all its bones in place is rare. Many fossils are found in what scientists call fossil graveyards. These fossil graveyards contain a mixture of many different kinds of fossils that have been *transported by large volumes of water* (see Figure 2).

Figure 2. Fossil Graveyard Example

The bones are typically fragments that have been broken apart during the transportation process as enormous mounds of mud and sediment were shifted during the Flood. By studying some of these fossil graveyards, we can gather clues that will demonstrate that the Flood was in fact catastrophic and worldwide, as stated in Genesis 7:20–23:

> The waters rose and covered the mountains to a depth of more than fifteen cubits [at least 22 feet]. *Every living thing* that moved on land perished—birds, livestock, wild animals, *all the creatures* that swarm over the earth, and *all mankind. Everything* on dry land that had the breath of life in its nostrils died. *Every living thing* on the face of the earth was wiped out; people and animals and the creatures that move along the ground and the birds were wiped from the earth. *Only Noah was left*, and those with him in the ark. (emphasis added)

If this passage in Genesis is true, we would expect to find *billions of dead things buried in rock layers laid down by water all over the Earth.*[23] And this is exactly what we find! In fact, such evidence exists *all over the world*. Next, we will discuss several example locations where mass Flood graves have been found.

Chilean Desert

There are at least 75 fossilized whales in the Chilean desert. One must ask: "How did they get there?" Even more amazing, the graveyard is located on top of a hill close to one half mile (a little less than a kilometer) from the Pacific Ocean. The whales "have been found in a roadside strip the length of two football fields—about 262 yards long and 22 yards wide."[24] Twenty of the whales were even found perfectly intact. Most scientists agree that the whales died at the same time, and for the same reason. But how did they die? A catastrophic flood such as Noah's Flood can certainly provide a possible explanation. Since they were deposited atop many miles of sedimentary rock layers that the Flood likely formed, this Chilean fossil graveyard might represent a pod of whales that got cut off from waters flowing off the newly rising South American continent probably during the latter months of the year-long Flood event.

Thousands of Buried Centrosaurs in Hilda, Canada

At least 14 dinosaur "bonebeds" rest in a region in Canada called Hilda. They contain thousands of buried Centrosaurs *found in the same stratigraphic column* (a term used in geology to describe the vertical location of rocks in a particular area). The authors who completed the most extensive study of the area described the sediment in which these dinosaurs are buried as "mudstone rich in organic matter deposited on the tract of land separating two ancient rivers."[25] They also concluded that each of the 14 bonebeds were actually parts of a single, massive "mega-bonebed" that occupied 2.3 square kilometers! Stop and think about this for a minute. How did thousands of dinosaurs—of the same species—get herded up and simultaneously buried in mud? These authors even concluded that the massive bonebed was formed when a herd of Centrosaurs *drowned during a flood*. These bonebeds are also found with aquatic vertebrates such as fish, turtles, and crocodiles, showing that water was definitely involved in their transport and burial. In addition, almost no teeth marks indicated any scavenging after these animals died (probably because most of them died at the same time!).

Massive Dinosaur Graveyard Found in China

An online article on Discovery.com describes the dinosaur graveyard in China as the largest in the world, writing, "Researchers say they can't understand why so many animals gathered in what is today the city of Zhucheng to die." Thousands of dinosaur bones have been found stacked on top of each other in "incredible density" right before they "suddenly vanished from the face of the Earth."[26] Most of the bones are found within a single 980-foot-long ravine in the Chinese countryside, about 415 miles southeast of Beijing. Clearly, processes were going on in the past so violent that we can only imagine them.

10,000+ Duck-billed Dinosaurs Buried Alive in Montana

In his article titled, "The Extinction of the Dinosaurs," Creation researcher Michael J. Oard describes some of the numerous dinosaur graveyards that are found all over the world.[27] He believes this is solid evidence of Noah's worldwide Flood. Oard reported that one of the largest bonebeds in the world is located in north-central Montana:

> Based on outcrops, an extrapolated estimate was made for 10,000 duckbill dinosaurs entombed in a thin layer measuring 2 km east-west and 0.5 km north-south. The bones are disarticulated and disassociated, and are orientated east-west. However, a few bones were standing upright, indicating some type of debris flow. Moreover, there are no young juveniles or babies in this bone-bed, and the bones are all from one species of dinosaur.

Two other scientists, Horner and Gorman, also described the bonebed: "How could any mud slide, no matter how catastrophic, have the force to take a two- or three-ton animal that had just died and smash it around so much that its femur—still embedded in the flesh of its thigh—split lengthwise?"[28] Oard concluded that a cataclysmic event is the best explanation for the arrangement of the bones.

Karoo Basin in South Africa

One of the most remarkable fossil graveyards is found in South Africa in a location known as the Karoo Basin. It was once estimated to contain 800 billion fossil remains. That number was shown to be an overestimation, but the fossils may still be in the billions.[29] Regardless, the fossil bed covers an area over 200,000 square miles, making it one of the largest fossil deposits on Earth.[30] The fossil debris contains many species of plants, insects, fish, reptiles and amphibians. Quite a mixture—everything stirred together as some catastrophic soup! The rock layers containing these fossils were most likely deposited towards the end of the Flood in the same kind of rock layers containing the petrified logs that make up the famous Painted Desert Formation of the Southwestern United States.

Redwall Limestone in the Grand Canyon

Another remarkable fossil graveyard bed and mass kill is located in a seven foot layer of what was once lime mud now hardened within the Redwall Limestone. The layer contains perhaps billions of cigar-shaped (orthocone) nautiloids.[31] Nautiloids are extinct today, but those with coiled shells resembled the chambered nautilus, a squid-like animal inside a shell. This single extensive bed covers an area of 11,583 square miles, about the size of the state of Maryland, and extends from the Grand Canyon in Arizona all the way to Las Vegas, Nevada, and overlaps into southern Utah. During the Flood, a widespread underwater mud flow wiped out these ocean-dwelling swimmers and deposited the mass kill towards the western edge of North America. Even today, underwater avalanches can cause fast-flowing wedges of muddy debris that cut through the ocean floor, but we have never observed them at the size of Maryland! Because of the slender conical shape of the nautiloid, they act like wind vanes. When the nautiloids exit the tumbling debris flow, some of the shells align with the direction of the current (i.e., the retreating Flood waters). A geologist can use this data to calculate direction of the torrential debris flow.

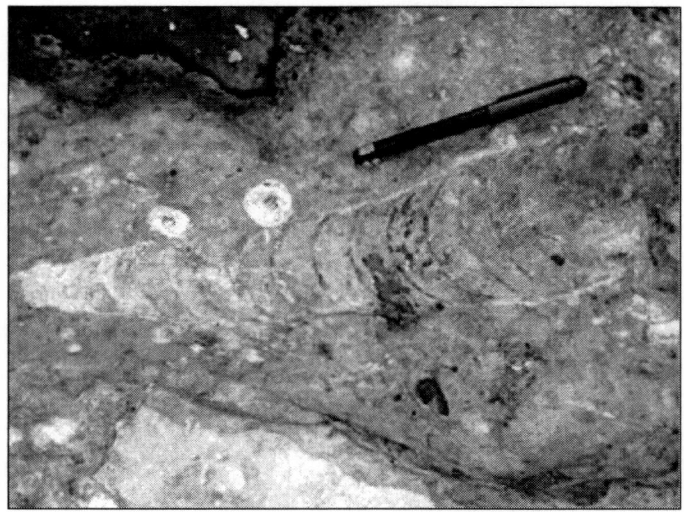

Figure 3. Nautiloid Indicating Flow Direction

Burgess Shale in the Canadian Rockies

The Burgess Shale in the Canadian Rockies at an elevation of 6,700 feet contains a remarkable collection of ancient fossilized life. Not only are the hard body parts such as bones, teeth, and shells preserved, but soft body tissue such as muscles, gills, and digestive systems are also fossilized (many "with soft parts intact, often with food still in their guts"[32]—making it obvious that they were immediately buried). It is rare to find soft body parts fossilized. It is important to understand that an animal or plant becomes a fossil only if it is buried rapidly. Scavengers would eat the animal if it were not completely buried immediately after it dies.

Another researcher remarks with the same findings: "The Burgess Shale is, therefore, an enormous fossil graveyard, produced by countless animals living on the sea floor being catastrophically swept away in landslide-generated turbidity currents, and then buried almost instantly in the resultant massive turbidite layers, to be exquisitely preserved and fossilized."[33]

Ordovician Soom Shale in South Africa

This massive fossil area is 30 feet thick, spans hundreds of miles, and contains thousands of exceptionally-preserved fossils.[34] The eurypterids even show "walking appendages that are normally lost to early decay after death" and "some of the fibrous muscular masses that operated these appendages."[35] Snelling continues: "The evidence is clearly consistent with catastrophic burial of countless thousands of these organisms over thousands of square kilometers, which implies that the shale itself had to be catastrophically deposited and covered under more sediments before burrowing organisms could destroy the laminations."[36]

Other Major Fossil Deposits

Still not convinced? Need more proof? The world contains many other fossil graveyards that include numerous types of animal and plant life. Ambitious readers are encouraged to explore these other fossil grounds, including:

- Green River Formation of Wyoming (alligators, fish, birds, turtles, clams, insects, a horse, lizards, lemur-like primates, squirrel-like mammals, ferns, and palm leaves).
- Montceau-les-Mines, France (hundreds of thousands of marine creatures were buried with amphibians, spiders, scorpions, millipedes, insects, and reptiles).[37]
- Mazon Creek area near Chicago (more than 400 species represented by over 100,000 fossils).
- Devonian Thunder Bay Limestone formation in Michigan (spans hundreds of miles and is over 12

feet thick in many places. Includes millions of fossils buried in the Flood).

- Carboniferous Francis Creek Shale in Illinois (fossil graveyard containing specimens representing more than 400 species).
- The Triassic Mont San Giorgio Basin in Italy and Switzerland ("Over 300 feet deep and about four miles in diameter, containing thousands of well-preserved fossils of fish and reptiles, including fossilized fish containing embryos inside their abdomens, and a fossilized Tanystropheus, a 4.5-meter giraffe-necked saurian, which also contains the remains of unborn young"[38]).
- Triassic Cow Brand Formation in Virginia (contains a mixture of fossilized terrestrial, freshwater, and marine plants, insects, and reptiles that were buried together in a massive graveyard).[39]
- The Cretaceous Santana Formation in Brazil (thousands of marine and land fossils, including sharks, crocodiles, and pterosaurs).
- Siwalki Hills north of Delhi, India (ranges 2,000 to 3,000 feet high and includes thousands of fossils).
- The Morrison Formation (one million square miles in 13 U.S. states and three Canadian provinces, including dinosaur bones fossilized together with fish, turtles, crocodiles, and mammals).
- Geiseltal in Germany (contains "a complete mixture of plants and insects from all climatic zones and all recognized regions of the geography of plants or animals"[40]).

Not too many fossils are being formed today. Only a worldwide catastrophic flood could produce the many fossil-bearing sediments and fossil graveyards we observe around the world today. Much of this evidence—particularly the fossils of the smaller, more delicate animals and soft tissue—stands in great contrast to Darwin's assertion that "No organism wholly soft can be preserved."[41] The only way to preserve countless millions of intricate fossils all over the world is to bury them quickly in mud and sediment! Even clams, which open after they die, are found around the world in fossil graveyards in the closed position, indicating they were buried rapidly.[42]

Coal Deposits

Evolutionists claim that coal deposits have been formed over millions of years. If this is true, David Cloud asks this compelling question: "How can they sometimes contain perfectly-preserved fossils, including two-ton dinosaurs, which would have to have been covered almost instantly? For example, in 1878, miners working in the Mons coalfield in Belgium discovered 39 iguanodon dinosaur skeletons, many of them complete, at a depth of 322 meters. They were 10 meters long and weighed two tons each. 'For their bodies to be rapidly buried would require rates of deposition thousands or even millions of times greater than the average 0.2 millimeters per year proposed by uniformitarians.'"[43]

During my college days, I had the opportunity to study several coal mines in western Kentucky. I was surprised to find evidence showing their rapid accumulation. This contradicts the swamp model which states it takes tens of millions of years of slow accumulation and burial of plant material before it will turn to coal. Between the layers of coal deposits we found layers of sandstone, limestone and clays, all containing marine fossils and plant material. Sedimentary structures in these layers indicated they were deposited in fast-moving waters. One coal bed was even cut or channeled by a deposit of sandstone.

Figure 4. Sandstone Channel Cutting Coal Beds in Western Kentucky

Because these coal beds associate with the upper and lower strata (a layer of sedimentary rock or soil), they were also deposited rapidly during a catastrophic event. This challenges the slow and gradual swamp model. Not only that, coal deposits do not have the deep-penetrating roots that swamp and peat soils have. The Flood formed coal beds as water action sorted plant debris.

Polystrate Fossils

In many coal and sediment deposits, fossilized trees are found standing in an upright position. These are called polystrate fossils because they are encased within and cross several layers of sedimentary rock.

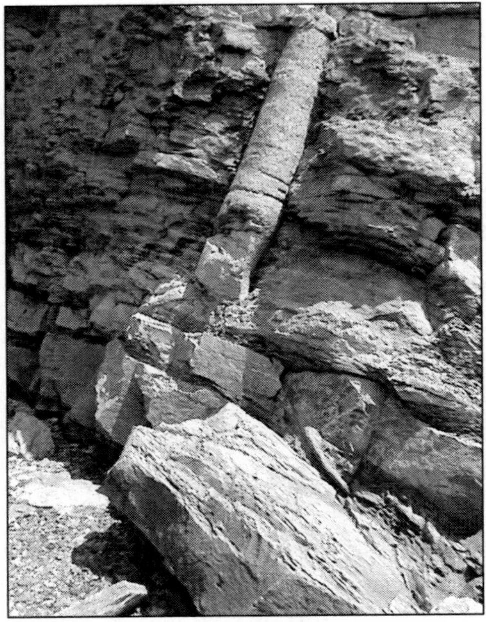

Figure 5. Polystrate Fossil Tree[44]

If the sandstone or clay was deposited very slowly, the trees would rot and not be preserved. The sediments had to rapidly bury the trees in order for them to stay upright and fossilize. Other kinds of fossils are buried and encased or extend into multiple layers of sediment. Dr John Morris notes, "I've seen hundreds of individual fossils whose body width exceeds the width of the banded layers in which they are encased."[45] It would be impossible for a dead fish or animal to stay in an upright position and be perfectly fossilized, with all parts intact, if the sediments accumulated slowly.

One such example is the "Kamikaze" ichthyosaur described by Tas Walker and Carl Wieland.[46] This ichthyosaur (an extinct dolphin-like marine reptile) was found "buried in a vertical, nose-down position at 90 degrees to the rock layers." Walker and Wieland continue: "Unlike most fossils, the head was preserved in three dimensions, and had not been flattened by the weight of sediment above it...The skull was enclosed vertically within three geological layers, which have been dated according to long-age beliefs, by reference to the fossils they contain. Curiously, the layers span an 'age' of about one million years, and that presents something of a problem for long-age geologists."

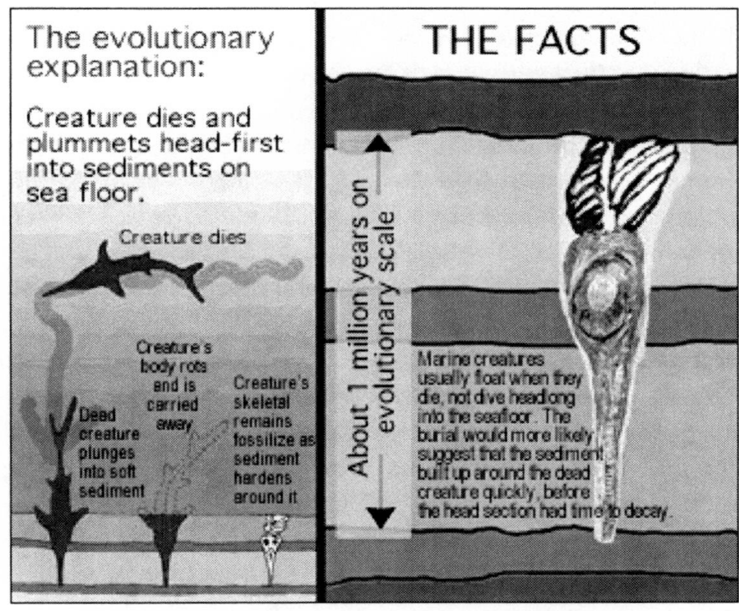

Figure 6. Ichthyosaur Head Spanning Three Layers (supposedly deposited over one million years)[47]

You don't have to be a fossil expert to see the problems with this situation. Just how can a complete ichthyosaur head be buried in a vertical position *slowly* over a million years? It is much more likely that this animal was killed and buried rapidly during Noah's Flood, and that all these layers formed at nearly the same time. There have also been several fossils recovered that were *in the process of giving birth*.[48]

The Earth's Sedimentary Rocks

The most common type of rock found on the Earth's surface is sedimentary rock deposited by water. We learn in the study of earth science that sedimentary rocks are made of broken pieces of preexisting rock. The clasts or pieces range from very small, such as those in mud, to large cobbles and even house-sized boulders. "Strata" is a term applied to layers of all types of sedimentary rocks. Many people don't realize that the sediments or strata were laid down and spread out over vast amounts of land surface. Some cover nearly the entire continent of North America. These are called blanket sandstones. Also the Earth's strata occur in six thick packages called megasequences. Each megasequence shares the same kind of material, clast patterns, and fossils which enables scientists to trace the sequence for long distances.

The Tapeats Sandstone is one of the lowest blanket sandstones. It was deposited at the start of the Flood in areas of North America. Evidence within the Tapeats strata, such as ripple beds and well-developed cross-beds, is consistent with rapid deposition. Cross-beds and ripples form when water currents are fast and strong.

Figure 7. Well Developed Cross-beds in Sandstone Indicates Rapidly Moving Waters

Additionally, large boulders are found at the base of the Tapeats Sandstone. This also shows that currents were strong and violent, ripping up and pulverizing the underlying bed rocks.

Another layer named the Redwall Limestone is found in the Grand Canyon and extends under other local names across America as far as Tennessee and Pennsylvania. The same kinds of sediments and fossils are even found across the Atlantic Ocean in England. Geologist Andrew Snelling states, "Every continent contains layers of sedimentary rocks that span vast areas. Many of these layers can even be traced across continents."[49] Only a world-covering flood could deposit such vast amounts of sediment as a single layer!

The Bible states that at the beginning of the Flood, "... all the fountains of the great deep burst open ..." (Genesis 7:11). Geologists have found deposits of large boulders and megabreccia beds—composed of very large angular fragments of rock laid down in a mud flow—that outcrop on the edges of most continents. The Kingston Peak Formation located in the Mojave Desert of California is a leading example of this type of deposit. These megabreccia beds are also found in Utah and Idaho, and extend into Canada as well. They show where the edge of the North American continent probably was at the start of the Flood.

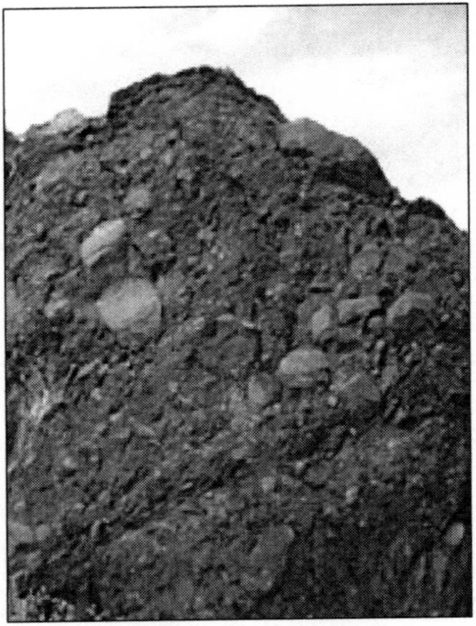

Figure 8. Megabreccia

These deposits were most likely laid down at the start of the Flood when the ancient continent broke apart.

Mountain Building

Many people I run into know that fossil deposits are found in the highest mountains on Earth. They consider, "How could fossils that once lived on the ocean floor be found in the world's tallest mountains?" Most elevated mountains of the world contain strata with marine and plant fossils. For example, whale fossils are found high in the Andes Mountains with other marine fossils such as clams and giant oysters.[50] The peak of Mount Everest contains fossil ammonites.

Figure 9. The Pyramidal Summit of Mt. Everest is Composed of Fossil Bearing Limestones

Other examples of fossils at high elevation include the Burgess Shale mentioned above, and the Matterhorn, which sits at 14,690 feet in the Swiss Alps. It is composed of sedimentary layers which contain marine fossils such as clams, oysters, and fish! Much of the sedimentary layers in these mountains are folded, tilted, and "cracked" (faulted) due to the tectonic forces that raised them. If these mountain ranges are tens of millions of years old then they shouldn't be as elevated. They should be worn down as hills or eroded away completely based on the current rate of erosion. In fact, subsequent research has verified what John Morris wrote in *The Young Earth: The Real History of the Earth, Past, Present, and Future* about how modern erosion rates would have erased all continents in 50 million years or so, since erosion occurs faster than uplift.

I've talked to many people who don't understand that most mountains were formed very recently in so-called geologic time. Geologic time is referred to as "deep time," and it starts at about 4.5 billion years ago. Of course, even as a geologist I am unconvinced of deep time, instead preferring the biblical time scale. If we searched the internet or textbooks for "mountain building" we would find that, on average, the tallest mountains started uplifting around 60 million years ago. So, assuming for argument the conventional age of the Earth as 4.5 billion years old and accepting geologic "deep time," let's compare geologic time to a twenty-four hour day. The 60 million year-old mountain building events would only take about the last eighteen minutes of a twenty-four hour day to appear. So, mountain building is a recent geologic event within the evolutionary time frame.

Now some scientists think, based on the fossils, that today's highest mountains are a lot younger than the 60 million years stated above.[51] Pliocene fossils, deposited about 5 million years ago using the conventional geologic time frame, are found in the Himalayas and Andes Mountains. So, compared to the twenty-four hour day above, these mountains appeared in the last two minutes of the day!

Bristlecone Pines

Consider the Bristlecone Pines, believed to be some of the oldest living organisms on the Earth. These hardy, twisted pines grow in arid regions of Western North America at altitudes between 5,600 and 11,200 feet. Researchers can estimate the ages of these trees by counting the "growth rings," which typically grow at a rate of one per year, but can grow more than one ring during wet years. One such Bristlecone Pine, called the "Methuselah" pine (named after the biblical character Methuselah, who lived to be 969 years old[52]), has an estimated age of 4,845 years. Just this year, an even older tree was found with an estimated age of 5,063.[53]

Figure 10. Bristlecone Pines on the tops of White Mountains, California

Is this just a coincidence that these trees are found on high elevated mountains? Or, could the Bristlecone pines have rooted at the end of the Flood on dry land and then have been uplifted during the mountain building process at that time? The fact that the Earth's oldest trees are found on the mountain tops fits well with recent mountain building episodes towards the end of the catastrophic Flood of Noah. The truth is that it makes more sense that the mountains rose *rapidly* at the end of the Flood—after the many ocean-dwelling animals were buried and fossilized (mostly clams) and seeds were sprouted. As mentioned earlier, given the current rate of mountain uplift and erosion, uplift had to be faster than erosion or the mountains would be worn away.

One must also ask the question: "Why are there no trees alive today that significantly exceed typical Flood date estimates (around 2350 B.C.)?" This is especially convincing given that several tree species have the ability to live longer than 6,000 years, but no such trees are found! In addition to the Bristlecone Pines discussed above, the giant sequoias in California can also live longer, but the oldest living sequoias can only be traced back about 3,200 years.[54] The answer is that these trees began their lives after the Flood.

Landscapes Formed by Catastrophic Processes

When the Flood waters drained from the Earth, many landscapes were formed that can't be explained by isolated local floods or slower processes supposedly occurring over thousands and even millions of years. These landscapes are referred to as erosional remnants or left-overs. They are not forming today. The list is long so we will discuss only some of the more obvious surface features. There are many elevated areas around the world that have very conspicuous flat-topped surfaces. The Colorado Plateau, for example, is made of several plateaus that range in elevation between 5,000 feet to 11,000 feet above sea level and covers an area of 130,000 square miles.

Figure 11. Western Edge of the Colorado Plateau East of Las Vegas, Nevada (notice peneplained surfaces on the plateau)

Most people are familiar with the plateaus, mesas, and buttes found in such places as Grand Canyon and Canyonlands National Park. Large volumes of receding Flood waters washed away thousands of feet of sediment, leaving relatively flat-lying surfaces forming these plateaus, mesas and buttes.

Figure 12. Canyonlands in Eastern Utah

These flat surfaces are called peneplains or planation surfaces and are only formed by strong currents of water spread over large areas. Peneplains are found worldwide and are not forming today.[55] The Beartooth Mountains of Montana and western Wyoming contain a remarkable peneplained surface at the summit that rises 12,000 feet above sea level.

Figure 13. Beartooth Mountains

These flat-topped surfaces are best explained by large-scale sheet erosion due to the retreating Flood waters that occurred as mountains were building.

In western North America, the many dry lake basins were filled with water and formed a network of connected lakes in the recent past. Ancient Lake Manley filled the Death Valley basin and connected with lakes found in the Mojave Desert to the south. The Great Salt Lake in Utah which covers an area of 1,700 square miles and average depth of sixteen feet looks large, but is actually much smaller than the lake that once occupied that territory. If ancient Lake Bonneville was around today it would have swallowed the Great Salt Lake and surrounding areas. Lake Bonneville was eleven times larger than Great Salt Lake and one thousand feet deep. The shorelines of the ancient lake are found 984 feet above the present lake level.

Figure 14. Great Salt Lake with Wasatch Mountains in the Background (when Lake Bonneville was around the lake level was about 1000 feet higher as recorded in the shore lines in the mountains)

What happened to the lake's water? Apparently, the natural dam that once held Lake Bonneville broke. It must have been terrible to witness the ancient catastrophe, as the lake discharged its huge volume of water towards the north, running over southeastern Idaho through the Snake River basin and out to the Pacific Ocean. It left an array of carved canyons in its wake.

Most river beds today are considered underfit because the current river or stream is too small to have eroded the valley in which it flows. Wide river channels or river valleys attest to the large amounts of water the river carried in the past. If we looked at the Snake River valley we would see that the current river does not fit the valley. The valley was formed rapidly by the catastrophic release of ancient Lake Bonneville. Many areas in Utah and Nevada show that large volumes of water drained from the land in the past. The Virgin River in Utah starts near Zion National Park, follows the Virgin River Gorge, and empties into Lake

Mead, Nevada. This is what we see in the modern landscape on Earth: evidence that in the past large volumes of water drained from the land. A world-encompassing flood could have filled ancient large lakes that later drained, producing the erosional remnant landscapes we see in western North America and worldwide.

Noah's Ark

If there was a worldwide Flood, then all life on Earth would have been blotted out. But today the planet teems with millions of plants and animals. Where did they come from? The Bible states that Noah built an Ark, Genesis 6:15. On board were his wife, his three sons with their wives, as well as animals of every kind. Some question the size of this boat, how many animals were on the boat, and how the animals repopulated Earth after the waters drained. These are good questions when asked by someone who genuinely wants answers. Let us answer each in turn.

The Bible gives us the dimensions of the Ark: 300 x 50 x 30 cubits. In ancient times, a cubit was measured by the length from a man's elbow to the tip of his fingers. Using the long or royal cubit definition, this translates to Ark dimensions of about 510 x 85 x 51 feet. Using a more conservative cubit of about 17.5 inches, the Ark would have been approximately 437.5 x 72.92 x 43.75 feet. This translates to a total volume of about 1,396,000 cubic feet. The inside dimensions of a 40-foot school bus gives about 2,080 cubic feet of space. Therefore, 671 school buses without their wheels and axels could fit inside of Noah's Ark. If each bus carried 50 students, then 33,550 kids could easily fit in the Ark. Wow! And there would even be enough room left over for food and other supplies. The Ark had plenty of room!

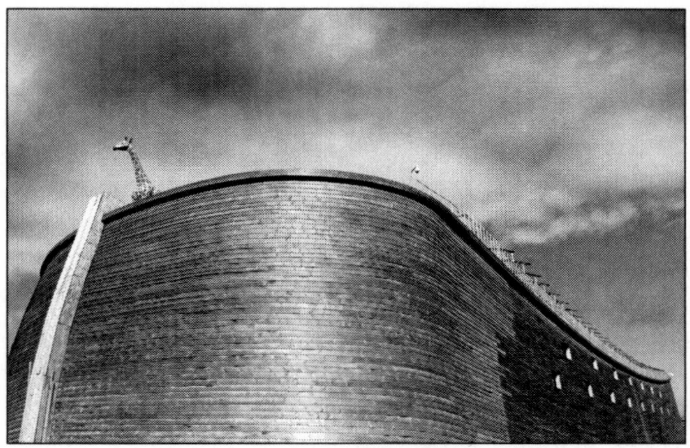

Figure 15. Life-size Replica of Noah's Ark (Built by John Huibers in Dordrecht, Netherlands)

Figure 16. Life-size Replica of Noah's Ark (Notice the giraffe on the front of the ship!)

Another interesting fact about the Ark is that God knew *exactly what He was doing* when He gave Noah the specific dimensions for building the Ark. In fact, in 1993, Dr. Seon Won Hong[56] conducted a scientific study to investigate the seaworthiness of the Ark at the renowned ship research center KRISO (now called MOERI) in South Korea.[57] After evaluating the seaworthiness of over 10 various ship dimensions, the study showed that the Ark dimensions given in the Bible were ideal for handling everything a highly turbulent sea could throw at it. In fact, this study showed that the Ark could handle 100-foot waves.

An earlier study conducted in the 17th Century by Peter Jansen of Holland showed that the length-to-width ratio of the Ark (about 6-to-1) was ideal for such a massive, non-powered sea vessel (some oil tankers are 7-to-1). He also demonstrated using replica models of the Ark that it was almost impossible to capsize.[58]

How Many Animals Were aboard the Ark?

Noah only took air-breathing, land-dwelling, animals with nostrils onto the Ark. Some marine creatures like fish and amphibians could survive the Flood. Some seeds would sprout and root various plants and trees, and Genesis 6:21 tells us that Noah brought plants and seeds onto the Ark as well. How many animals were there? There are many estimates as to this number. First, it is important to understand that not every species (under most current definitions of this term) had to be on the Ark—only pairs of each animal *kind*. Equating "kind" with the standard "genus" names overestimates the number at 8,000 kinds.[59] A basic kind of animal for example would be a dog or cat. There are many different kinds of dogs today but Noah only had to take two dogs, a male and a female (e.g., wolves, coyotes, and domestic dogs can inter-breed and represent the same "kind").

Taking two of each "kind" means that no more than 16,000 animals had to be on the Ark to reproduce the animal life we see today. What about those few animals that grew to great sizes, like sauropod dinosaurs? Rather than bringing large animals that may have passed their reproductive primes, it is likely that Noah brought younger adolescent animals on the Ark. All the animals, a large measure of which were probably bird kinds, averaged about the size of a sheep.[60] Reflecting on our school bus comparison, a lot of small animals could fit on the Ark with room to spare.

After the Flood, dry land appeared[61] and the animals left the Ark to repopulate the Earth. The climate and geographical conditions must have changed drastically. So, the basic kinds of animals would have to adapt to different environments. This is what scientists see today. The same kind of animal can adapt to a different environment by changing certain characteristics. For example, some birds can change the size and shape of their beak in order to eat certain nuts or insects. The bird hasn't changed into a different kind of animal such as a reptile, and it hasn't even generated a non-bird body feature. It is still a bird with a different size and shape beak. This process has generated from the original "kinds" that left the Ark—the many different animal and plant varieties we see today.

The drastic climate changes that occurred after the Flood also led to humans living shorter lives,[62] the ice age,[63] and many of the dinosaurs that survived the Flood via the Ark to go extinct faster than many other animals (e.g., due to the scarce food supply and increased competition for habitat).[64]

Conclusion

Only a catastrophic, worldwide flood could deposit thousands of feet of sedimentary rock layers that almost covered whole continents. Within these sediments, billions of dead animals were buried and fossilized, just as we would expect from the Bible's Flood account. Late Flood upheavals lifted some of these sedimentary rocks with their fossils to the highest peaks in the world for all to see. Continents, fossils, and mountains are what we would expect to see if there really was a worldwide Flood as described in Genesis.

Chapter 3:

The Age of the Earth, Dating Methods, and Evolution

Roger Sigler, M.S.

Why is this Chapter Important?

This chapter is important because an "ancient Earth" is foundational to evolutionary theory. As one high school biology textbook states: "Evolution takes a long time. If life has evolved, then Earth must be very old...Geologists now use radioactivity to establish the age of certain rocks and fossils. This kind of data could have shown that the Earth is young. If that had happened, *Darwin's ideas would have been refuted and abandoned*. Instead, radioactive dating indicates that Earth is about 4.5 billion years old—plenty of time for evolution and natural selection to take place"[65] (emphasis added).

Thus, biology and earth science textbooks today will admit that "billions" (for the Earth) and "millions" (for life on Earth) of years are necessary for evolutionary theory to hold up. These books use these "ancient" dating ideas to assert that fossils are proof of biological evolution. What we will find out in this Chapter, however, is that the age of

God's Creation is younger than these textbooks state, and that the dating methods used to establish the "old Earth" are flawed in many respects.

Overview

Fossil remains are found in sedimentary rock layers. Layers of sediment are formed when various size particles (e.g., dirt, rocks, and vegetation) accumulate in places such as deserts, rivers, lakes, and the ocean. Most texts teach that it takes a long time for these sediments to build up, with older layers buried beneath younger layers. Fossils found in lower layers are deemed to be older than those in the upper layers, older on the bottom younger on the top. This is called relative age dating. To help establish the relative ages of rock layers and their fossils, evolutionary scientists use *index fossils*.

Index fossils are distinct fossils, usually an extinct organism, used to establish and correlate the relative ages of rock layers. Index fossils have a short stratigraphic or vertical range, which means they are found in only a few layers, though in many widespread places. Evolutionists assume that the creature evolved somehow, lived for a certain time period, and then died out. Textbooks are correct when they state that relative dating provides no information whatsoever about a fossil's absolute age. Nevertheless, most textbook writers and the scientists they cite all grew up with a belief in uniformitarian geologic processes. The principle of uniformity is a philosophy and an assumption that the slow geologic processes going on today is how the deposits of the past happened, or that the present is the key to the past. This assumption works well enough only for recent deposits such as the Quaternary and certain formations in the Tertiary periods (see Figure 17). But if you really want to learn, keen observations in the field testify that the rock layers were laid down catastrophically.

What you are not being told is that many sedimentary deposits from most of the periods in the Paleozoic and Mesozoic eras are primarily marine, very extensive, and bear great evidence of very fast or catastrophic depositional processes. Fossils in pristine condition require that the animal or plant was buried rapidly; therefore, index fossils, rather than indicating a living environment over time, are nothing more than things buried quickly and suffocated under huge amounts of sediments transported by the ocean. Another thing is that these widespread oceanic deposits occur hundreds and even thousands of miles inland from the ocean. Furthermore, these marine sediments sit above granitic crust, composed primarily of granite and related rocks. Granite, by its very nature, floats so as to be a foundation for land, not the ocean.

At the present time the ages shown on the geologic time scale are based on radiometric age dating. In many textbooks, radiometric ages are considered absolute ages. But as you will soon learn, it is far from absolute as far as dating goes, though is useful for other things. By reading this chapter, you will learn the truth and know more about the evidences for a young Earth than most adults. You will discover why the land, sea, and air are young; how dinosaur bones and other fresh fossils are young; and why diamonds belched from the bowels of the Earth were made fast and are young, even though all of these things originated as living things on the Earth's surface! So let's get started.

The Age of the Earth

The alleged age of the Earth is based on an interpretation of its radioactivity. The planet itself is given an age of 4.5 billion years and the various rock layers are given names with assigned ages (Figure 17). In many textbooks, radiometric ages are considered absolute ages. In reality, the ages are far from absolute. To understand exactly why, we must first learn the basics of radioactive elements, and of the techniques used when treating these systems of elements as clocks.

The ages of the geologic periods shown in Figure 17 are based primarily on radioactive isotopes. Many elements on the periodic table have radioactive forms. Stable atoms have a set number of protons, neutrons, and orbital electrons. Isotopes are atoms of the same elements with the same number of protons but different numbers of neutrons, so these atoms are radioactive. This means its nucleus is not stable and will change or transmutate into another element over time by emitting particles and/or radiation.

EON	ERA	PERIOD	EPOCH	Alleged Age Years	Young Earth Evidences
Phanerozoic (This is where most fossils occur)	Cenozoic	Quaternary	Holocene	10,000	
			Pleistocene	2,600,000	Soft Frog with bloody bone marrow
		Tertiary	Pliocene	5,300,000	⇐ Salamander muscle
			Miocene	23,000,000	
			Oligocene	30,900,000	⇐ Young coal, Penguin feathers, Lizard skin
			Eocene	55,800,000	
			Paleocene	65,500,000	
	Mesozoic	Cretaceous		145,500,000	⇐ Young Diamonds Young Coal
		Jurassic		201,600,000	Dinosaur DNA, blood, blood vessels and protein
		Triassic		251,000,000	
	Paleozoic	Permian		299,000,000	
		Pennsylvanian		318,000,000	⇐ Young Coal
		Mississippian		359,000,000	
		Devonian		416,000,000	
		Silurian		444,000,000	
		Ordovician		488,000,000	
		Cambrian		542,000,000	
Precambrian	Proterozoic Eon			2,500,000,000	⇐ Helium in zircon crystals
	Archean Eon			3,850,000,000	

Figure 17. Uniformitarian Geologic Time Scale (with problems noted)

Uniformitarian Geologic Time Scale modified after the Geological Society of America, 2009. The time scale is placed vertically because older sedimentary deposits are buried beneath younger sedimentary deposits. The assumption of slow geologic processes and radiometric age dating has drastically inflated the age of the Earth and its strata.

A basic way to measure the rate of radioactive decay is called the half-life. This is the length of time needed for 50% of a quantity of radioactive material to decay. Unstable radioactive isotopes called parent elements decay (or give birth to) stable elements called daughter elements. Each radioactive element has its own specific half-life (see Table 5).

Table 5: Radiometric Isotopes and Half Lives

Examples of Radioactive Isotopes that Change into Stable Elements		
Radioactive Parent Element	**Stable Daughter Element**	**Half-Life**
Carbon-14 (^{14}C)	Nitrogen-14 (^{14}N)	5,730 Years
Potassium-40 (^{40}K)	Argon-40 (^{40}Ar)	1.3 Billion Years
Uranium-238 (^{238}U)	Lead-206 (^{206}Pb)	4.5 Billion Years
Rubidium-87 (^{87}Rb)	Strontium-87 (^{87}Sr)	48.6 Billion Years

Note: Carbon 14 is not used to date minerals or rocks, but is used for organic remains that contain carbon, such as wood, bone, or shells.

To find the age of a rock, geologists review the ratio between radioactive parent and stable daughter products in the rock or in particular minerals of the rock. Igneous rocks—those that have formed from molten magma or lava—are the primary rock types analyzed to determine radiometric ages. For example, let's assume that when an igneous rock solidified, a certain mineral in it contained 1000 atoms of radioactive potassium (^{40}K) and zero atoms of argon (^{40}Ar). After one half-life of 1.3 billion years, the rock would contain 500 ^{40}K and 500 ^{40}Ar atoms, since 50% has decayed. This is a 500:500 or 500 parent/500 daughter ratio, which reduces to 1:1 or 1/1 ratio. If this was the case, then the rock would be declared to be 1.3 billion years old. If the ratio is greater than 1/1, then not even one half-life has expired, so the rock would be younger. But if the ratio is less than 1/1, then the rock is considered older than the half-life for that system (see Figure 18).

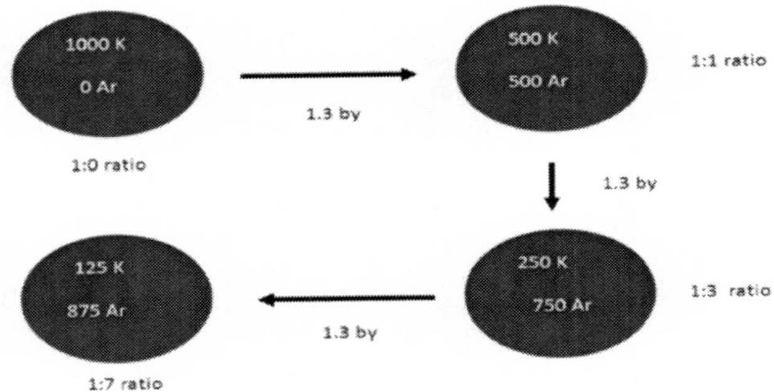

Figure 18. Decay of Radioactive potassium-40 to argon-40

Decay of Radioactive potassium-40 to argon-40. "BY" means "billions of years," K is potassium, Ar is argon. After three half-lives of this system, totaling 3.9 billion years, only 125 of the original set of 1000 radioactive potassium-40 atoms remain, assuming that the system has decayed evenly for all that time.

Dating a rock requires four basic assumptions:

1. Laboratory measurements that have no human error or misjudgments;
2. The rock began with zero daughter element atoms;
3. The rock maintained a "closed system;" (defined below) and
4. The decay rate remained constant.

Let's describe each of these. Measuring the radioactive parent and stable daughter elements to obtain the ratio between them must be accurate, and it usually is. But keep in mind that most laboratory technicians in dating labs have been trained in a belief of an old Earth, which may set preconceived ideas about the time periods they expect. They all memorized the typical geologic time scale, and thus may not have an open mind to the idea that the accurately measured isotope ratios may have come from processes other than radioisotope decay.

Next, this technician assumes that all the radioactive parent isotopes began decaying right when the mineral crystallized from a melt. He also assumes none of the stable daughter element was present at this time. How can anyone claim to know the mineral really began with 100% radioactive parent and 0% daughter elements? What if some stable daughter element was already present when the rock formed?

A closed system means that no extra parent or daughter elements have been added or removed throughout the history of the rock. Have you ever seen an atom? Of course not. It is really microscopic, but we must think about this assumption on an atomic level. For example, decay byproducts like argon and helium are both gases. Neither gas tends to attach to any other atom, meaning they are rarely involved in chemical reactions. Instead of reacting with atoms in rock crystals, they build up in rock systems and can move in and out of the rocks. In fact, a leading expert in isotope geology states that most minerals do not even form in closed systems. He emphasizes that for a radioactive-determined date to be true, the mineral must be in a closed system.[66] Is there any such thing as a closed system when speaking of rocks?

The constant-decay rate assumption involves the decay rate remaining the same throughout the history of the rock. Lab experiments have shown that most changes in temperature, pressure, and the chemical environment have very little effect on decay rates. These experiments have led researchers to have great confidence that this is a reasonable assumption, but it may not hold true. Is the following quote an overstatement of known science? "Radioactive transmutations must have gone on at the present rates under all the conditions that have existed on Earth in the geologic past."[67] Some scientists have found incredible evidence in zircon minerals showing that radioactive decay rates were much higher in the past.

Some of these assumptions are analogous to walking into a room where "...there is a burning candle sitting on the table. How long has that candle been burning? This can be calculated if the candle's *burn rate* and *original length* is known. However, if the original length is not known, or if it cannot be verified that the burning rate has been constant, it is impossible to tell for sure how long the candle was burning. A similar problem occurs with radiometric dating of rocks. Since the initial physical state of the rock is unknowable, the age can only be estimated according to certain assumptions."[68]

Helium and Accelerated Decay Rate

The amount of radiometric decay that has happened in igneous rocks like granite containing the mineral zircon is most often calculated by measuring the amount of radioactive uranium-238 and the amount of stable lead-206 within a given crystal. Decaying uranium-238 forms eight helium atoms on its way to becoming Lead-206. The helium atoms are temporarily trapped within the zircon crystal, which is considered about as closed a system as possible in the world of minerals. However, helium atoms are small, very lightweight, fast-moving, and do not form chemical bonds that would lock them with other atoms. They can therefore leak out of solids and into the atmosphere by passing through microscopic cracks in minerals, or by diffusing right through the solid walls of the mineral itself; that is, through the spaces in the crystal's net-like atomic arrangement. Think of a crystalline atomic lattice as a cage made of chain-link fencing. Dogs remain trapped in the cage, but squirrels can pass through the spaces. Helium atoms are like the small animals. They can squeeze through the spaces of the atomic lattice. Have you ever wondered why those helium balloons given at parties do not stay afloat for very long? It's because the helium atoms leak through the rubber.

In the 1970s, Los Alamos National Laboratories collected core samples of the Jemez granodiorite. It is considered a Precambrian granitic rock and bears an assigned age of 1.5 billion years based on uranium-238 – lead-206 dating. The rate of helium that leaks out or diffuses through the granodiorite was then measured at an internationally renowned laboratory. By dividing the amount of helium left in the rock with the measured diffusion rate of helium through the zircon crystals and other nearby minerals (e.g., mica), it is possible to measure how long ago the radioactive decay happened—as long as we make the required assumptions. This is the same concept as measuring the age of a helium balloon by knowing the amount of helium left in it and dividing by the rate at which the helium left the balloon. Amazingly, the radiometric decay that generated the helium within these zircon crystals had to have happened within the last 6000 +/-2000 years. There is no known mechanism which could have forced the helium to remain within these rocks for a longer period of time.

So here is the great mystery: One clock is based on the decay of one parent isotope uranium-238 into two daughter products, lead-206 and helium. The other clock is based on the rate that the helium produced from the decay diffuses through the mineral zircon. Since helium is therefore tightly coupled to the U-238 to Pb-206 decay process, nobody expected to find much helium in the rock believed to be 1.5 billion years old. However, the high concentrations of helium in the zircons show that the helium production time period must have been short and the nuclear decay process must therefore have been greatly accelerated. This would also explain why there just simply is not enough radioactively produced helium in the atmosphere to account for billions of years of decay.

Helium in the Atmosphere

Some of the helium produced from the U-238 – Pb-206 decay process enters the atmosphere from the Earth's crust. It quickly rises through the lower atmosphere like letting go of a helium-filled party balloon. The estimated rate is 2,000,000 atoms/cm^2/second. But forces such as gravity, escape velocity, and changes in temperature and density in the upper atmosphere significantly reduce the rate that helium atoms can escape into outer space. The amount of helium that escapes into outer space is estimated to be only 50,000 atoms/cm^2/second. If the Earth's atmosphere had zero helium when it was formed, then today's measured amount of 1.1×10^{20} atoms/cm^2 would have been produced in just 2 million years.[69] This is about 500 times younger than the secular age of most granitic rocks, and more than 2,000 times younger than the evolutionary age of the Earth.

Brand New Rocks Give Old "Ages"

There is now a great abundance of evidence in the science literature about rocks giving ages much older than they really are. Warnings go back to the late 1960s and 1970s, but most of the scientific community is still not paying attention. Radiogenic argon and helium contents of recent basalt lava erupted on the deep ocean floor from the Kilauea volcano in Hawaii were measured. Researchers calculated up to 22,000,000 years for brand new rocks![70] The problem is common (see Table 6).

Table 6: Young Volcanic Rocks with Really Old Whole-Rock K-Ar Model Ages [71]

Lava Flow, Rock Type, and Location	Year Formed or Known Age	^{40}K-^{40}Ar "Age"
Kilauea Iki basalt, Hawaii	A.D. 1959	8,500,000 years
Volcanic bomb, Mt. Stromboli, Italy	A.D. 1963	2,400,000 years
Mt. Etna basalt, Sicily	A.D. 1964	700,000 years
Medicine Lake Highlands obsidian, Glass Mountains, California	<500 years	12,600,000 years
Hualalai basalt, Hawaii	A.D. 1800–1801	22,800,000 years
Mt. St. Helens dacite lava dome, Washington	A.D. 1986	350,000 years

The oldest real age of these recent volcanic rocks is <500 years. But most are even much younger than this; people witnessed the molten lava solidify into rock just decades ago. In fact, many of these were only about 10 years old or less when tested. And yet ^{40}K-^{40}Ar dating gives ages from 350,000 to >22,800,000 years.

Potassium-Argon (^{40}K-^{40}Ar) has been the most widespread method of radioactive age-dating for the Phanerozoic rocks, where most of the fossils are. The initial condition assumption is that there was no radiogenic argon (^{40}Ar) present when the igneous rock formed. But just like the helium problem, there is too much (^{40}Ar) present in recent lava flows, so the method gives excessively old ages for recently formed rocks. The argon amounts in these rocks indicate they are older than their known ages. Could the argon have come from a source other than radioactive potassium decay? If so, then geologists have been trusting a faulty method.

These wrong radioisotope ages violate the initial condition assumption of zero (0%) radioactive argon present when the rock formed. Furthermore, there was insufficient time since cooling for measurable amounts of ^{40}Ar to have accumulated in the rock, due to the slow radioactive decay of ^{40}K. Therefore, radiogenic Argon (^{40}Ar) was *already present* in the rocks as they formed.

Radiometric age dating should no longer be sold to the public as providing reliable absolute ages. Excess argon invalidates the initial condition assumption for potassium dating, and excess helium invalidates the closed-system assumption for uranium dating. The ages shown on the uniformitarian geologic time scale should be removed.

Coal Deposits Are Young

Carbon dating is used for organic materials such as wood, bone, and other materials that contain carbon, not inorganic rocks. Radioactive carbon or carbon-14 (^{14}C) has been found in coal and other ancient materials deep in the geologic record. Given the short ^{14}C half-life of 5,730 years, organic materials purportedly older than 100,000 years (nearly 18 half-lives) should contain absolutely no detectable ^{14}C.[72]

Recall that the way scientists use radioisotope dating is by first measuring the ratio of radioactive parent versus stable versions of an element. Carbon dating works a bit differently, instead basing an age calculation on the ratio of radioactive carbon (^{14}C) to normal carbon (^{12}C). Carbon-14 decays to nitrogen, not carbon. Using a formula that compares that ratio, called the "percent modern carbon" or "pMC" in a sample to a standard modern pMC ratio, scientists calculate carbon ages for carbon-containing materials.

Astonishing discoveries over the past 30 years come from highly sensitive Accelerator Mass Spectrometer (AMS) methods used to test organic samples show measurable amounts of ^{14}C from every portion of the fossil-bearing rock layers all around North America (see Table 7).

Table 7: Carbon in Coal Deposits[73]

Coal Seam Name	Location	Geologic Interval of Deposition	$^{14}C/C$ (pMC)
Bottom	Freestone County, TX	Eocene	0.30
Beulah	Mercer County, ND	Eocene	0.20
Pust	Richland County, MT	Eocene	0.27
Lower Sunnyside	Carbon County, UT	Cretaceous	0.35
Blind Canyon	Emery County, UT	Cretaceous	0.10
Green	Navajo County, AZ	Cretaceous	0.18
Kentucky #9	Union County, KY	Pennsylvanian	0.46
Lykens Valley #2	Columbia County, PA	Pennsylvanian	0.13
Pittsburgh	Washington County, PA	Pennsylvanian	0.19
Illinois #6	Macoupin County, IL	Pennsylvanian	0.29

The percentage of modern carbon (pMC) ranges (0.10–0.46) in the coal seams corresponds to radiocarbon ages roughly from 40,000 to 60,000 carbon years. But the conventional interval from the bottom of the Pennsylvanian layers to the top of the Eocene layers spans many millions of years, from 318,000,000 to 34,000,000 years. So which age are we supposed to believe, that coal is hundreds of millions, tens of millions, or only tens of thousands of years old? Maybe all are wrong.

Furthermore, $^{14}C/C$ ratios have about the same average amount of pMC regardless of the supposed geologic ages assigned to them. For Pennsylvanian coal, the average is 0.27; for Cretaceous coal, the average is 0.21; and for Eocene coal, the average is 0.26. These all show about the same pMC. What might this consistency indicate? It looks like the plant debris that eventually became coal was uprooted or died at about the same time. There is no doubt that the tectonic upheaval that occurred during Noah's Flood did this when the fountains of the great deep ruptured according to Genesis 7:11. The dead plant debris then floated and sank at different weeks during the Flood and in some number of years afterwards as geologic processes of the Earth steadily stabilized. As a result of this cataclysmic Flood, continuous deposition of huge amounts of sediments compressed the plant debris into coal seams in various stratigraphic levels.

Not only have scientists discovered young-looking, still radioactive carbon in coal, but also in fossils including wood, amber, dinosaur bones, and other Earth materials like the one we discuss next.

Diamonds Are Forever Young

Equally as remarkable as radioactive carbon in coal is the presence of ^{14}C in diamonds. Diamonds are almost purely carbon. These gorgeous crystals and the mineral inclusions trapped inside them when growing give evidence they formed at great depths. Based on the types of mineral inclusions, diamonds now sampled and mined at or near the Earth's surface originated under extreme temperatures and pressures deep within the Earth, at depths from around 200 km to over 1000 km.[74]

Recently, diamonds were discovered that contain isotopically light organic carbon. This means that the carbon originated by photosynthesis on the Earth's surface. The organic carbon from some living things (maybe algae?) that died ended up on the ocean floor, and was then subducted along with oceanic crust deep into the mantle. The authors of one technical study wrote that "subducted organic carbon can retain its isotopic signature even into the lower mantle."[75] They estimate that the diamonds formed at a depth of about 1000 km (600 miles) or so based on mineral inclusions within them.

Table 8: Carbon in Diamonds from Kimberlite Pipes[76]

Kimberlite Pipe	Location	Geologic Interval of Eruption	$^{14}C/C$ (pMC)
Kimberley-1	Kimberley, South Africa	Cretaceous	0.02
Orapa-A	Orapa mine, Botswana, Africa	Cretaceous	0.01
Orapa-F	Orapa mine, Botswana, Africa	Cretaceous	0.03
Letlhakane-1	Letlhakane mine, Botswana, Africa	Cretaceous	0.04
Letlhakane-3	Letlhakane mine, Botswana, Africa	Cretaceous	0.07

Then, mainly during the Cretaceous interval during the Flood, explosive eruptions all around the world brought the diamonds up from these great deep places back to the Earth's surface, where they are now found in unique igneous structures called kimberlite pipes. Even some jewelry television commercials assert the whole process takes about a billion years or so. But like coal, there should not be any detectable carbon-14, if diamonds are really that old.

And yet, diamonds from five different mines in Africa were studied (Table 8). The diamonds contain measurable radioactive carbon-14 with an average of 0.03–0.04 pMC, which equates to roughly 65,000 radiocarbon years.[77] These diamonds were supposed to have formed long before the Cretaceous eruption, supposedly 145,500,000 years ago. The 65,000-year time period is a tiny fraction of time compared to the imaginary inflated age of 145,500,000 years. Radioactive carbon in pre-Cretaceous diamonds clearly refutes the millions-of-years age assignment for Cretaceous materials as well as the supposed billion years to make diamonds.

Fresh Meat in Old Rocks

Recent discoveries of fresh tissues within fossils all around the world are quite surprising to paleontologists who assume that Earth's strata formed over millions of years of deposition. If the rock layers are really millions of years old, then fresh proteins, DNA, and cell tissue should no longer exist.

In the Yunnan Province, China, researchers discovered protein in sauropod dinosaur embryos found in fossil eggs supposedly 190,000,000 years old. These proteins don't even last one million years. The presence of apatite, the mineral component that vertebrate animals and man manufacture into bone, found interwoven with embryonic bone tissue proves that the protein originated from organic matter directly from the dinosaurs.[78]

Exceptionally preserved sauropod eggshells discovered in Upper Cretaceous deposits in Patagonia, Argentina, contain young-looking tissues of embryonic titanosaurid dinosaurs. Since these original dinosaur proteins decay very rapidly, the scientists involved in the study imagined that "virtually instantaneous mineralization of soft tissues" (mineralization occurs when the bone material is replaced by minerals from the soil) somehow preserved them for millions of years.[79] But repeated lab studies show that even mineralized proteins don't last longer than hundreds of thousands of years. Mineralization may have been rapid enough to retain fragments of original biomolecules in these specimens. Retaining is reasonable, but calling upon mineralization to preserve proteins for millions of years is unscientific. Their results demonstrate that organic compounds and other biological structures still look similar to those found in modern eggshells, showing that perhaps only thousands of years have elapsed since the dinosaur eggs were catastrophically buried by flood sediments.

In addition to these two examples, dozens of discoveries have been reported in several scientific journals, primarily from the 1990s to the present. Here are a few of the incredible fresh finds along with their conventional ages in millions of years (MY):

- Salamander muscle, 18MY
- Intact soft Frog with bloody bone marrow, 10MY
- Ichthyosaur skin, 190MY
- Hadrosaur blood vessels, 80MY
- Archaeopteryx feather proteins, 150MY
- Mosasaur blood protein fragments, >65MY
- Penguin feathers, 36MY
- Scorpion shell including shell protein, 240MY

- Psittacosaurus skin, 125MY
- DNA from Hadrosaur bone cell nuclei, 65MY
- Lizard tail skin proteins, 40MY
- Type I collagen proteins (and whole connective tissues including elastin and laminin) from Tyrannosaurus Rex and Hadrosaur dinosaurs[80]

Think about this list for a moment. The idea that a frog, still soft with still-bloody-red colored bone marrow is 10,000,000 years old is preposterous. First of all, just to preserve soft body parts requires rapid burial. But even when buried in sediments, can fresh meat such as a soft frog, skin, proteins, blood, muscle tissue, and DNA really last for millions of years? Almost all the relevant laboratory decay studies demonstrate otherwise. The truth is that proteins, even locked inside bone tissue, have a maximum shelf life between 200,000 to 700,000 years in an optimal burial environment, and DNA molecules in bone are estimated to be undetectable after about 10,000 years.[81] Genuine, original body molecules and tissues show that fossils are maybe thousands, but not millions of years old. Can you find any of this scientific data in your biology textbook?

The Young Ocean

Evolutionists believe the ocean to be 3,000,000,000 years—that's 3 billion years—old. But the sodium (Na+) content of the ocean has been increasing. The processes which add and remove dissolved sodium to and from the seawater of the ocean have been well known for many decades (Table 9). Scientists can use this data to estimate maximum age ranges for oceans.

Table 9: Present Day Sodium Inputs and Outputs of Sodium to/from the Oceans[82]

Sodium (Na+) Added to the Ocean		**Sodium (Na+) Removed from Ocean**	
Process	**Amount x 10^{10} kg/ year**	**Process**	**Amount x 10^{10} kg/year**
Rivers	19.2	Sea Spray	6.0
Ocean Sediments	11.5	Cation Exchange	3.5
Groundwater from Continents	9.6	Burial of Pore Water in Sea Floor Sediments	2.2
Glacial Activity	4.0	Alteration of Basalt	0.44
Sea Floor Vents	1.1	Zeolite formation	0.08
Atmosphere, Volcanism, Marine Coastal Erosion	0.3	Halite Deposition	<0.004
Total Input Rate	**45.7**	**Total Output Rate**	**12.2**

Only about 1/4 (12.2/45.7) of the present amount of sodium added to the ocean can be accounted for by known removal processes. This indicates that the sodium concentration of the ocean is not in equilibrium, but continues to increase. The increase in sodium is Input minus Output or 45.7 -12.2 = 33.5 x 10^{10} kg/year (Table 9). There is no way that this much added salt can be reconciled with a 3-billion-year-old ocean. The enormous imbalance shows that the ocean should contain *much more salt* if the ocean is really that old.

In 1990, the total amount of sodium in the ocean was estimated at 1.47×10^{19} Kg. The present-day increase of sodium to the oceans is 3.35×10^{11} kg/year (same as 33.5×10^{10} in above paragraph). If we begin with zero sodium–an ocean of pure fresh water–then the time to fill the ocean with sodium is 1.47×10^{19} / 3.35×10^{11} kg/year = 43,880,597 years or about 44 million years. This can be stretched to a maximum age of 62 million years when reduced input rates and maximum output rates are used.

But this does not mean the ocean is 44 to 62 million years old. The ocean must be much younger than this, since most ocean creatures need at least a little salt in their environment. Remember, the maximum age of 62 million years assumes that the ocean started as fresh water with 0% sodium and with no global catastrophic additions of sodium. Obviously, the original ocean contained a certain amount of sodium, making it far younger.

Just like sodium, rivers carry most of the sediments eroded from the continents into the ocean basins. The worldwide average depth of all the sediments on the seafloor is less than 1200 feet. More than 24,000,000,000 metric tons is dumped into the oceans each year. Only 1,000,000,000 tons of these deposits are dragged below the crust by tectonic plate subduction each year, which equates to 23,000,000,000 metric tons that accumulate on the seafloor. At this present rate, all these sediments would accumulate in only about 12,000,000 years into an empty ocean.[83]

Since the ocean is not likely to have begun as pure fresh water, the maximum age of 62,000,000 years based on salt content has been reduced to 12,000,000 years based on sediment input. But 12,000,000 years represents a maximum age limit because this assumes a completely empty ocean at the start and is based on present rates of deposition from the rivers.

In the biblical creation model, perhaps most of the sodium was added to the ocean by rapid geologic processes during creation, to support the marine life in the first place. God created the oceans on Day 3 to be inhabited on Day 5. Later, Noah's Flood rapidly dumped who knows how much salt and sediment from its reworked continents into the ocean.

All the world's ocean floors look very young. They most likely resulted from catastrophic plate tectonic activity during the Flood.[84] When the floodwaters rapidly drained off emerging continents, the erosion and sedimentation rates into the oceans would have been exponentially greater than the present rate of accumulation. This is because the enormous ocean itself was receding off the continents at first. The volume of water and sediments carried back to the oceans was drastically higher during this receding process. In addition, perhaps more than a dozen "megafloods," like the one that carved the English Channel and another that carved Washington State's Snake River basin, catastrophically drained to quickly add more sediment during the post-Flood Ice Age. These events elevated sea level by 300 or so feet worldwide as tremendous ice sheets and glaciers melted over several centuries. Eventually it gave way to the lower amount of river sedimentation observed today. Thus, the best interpretation is that all the sediments on the ocean floor accumulated in just a few to several thousand years ago, since the Flood.

Summary of Young Earth Evidence

Why don't standard school textbooks include these solid scientific reasons and observations that refute conventional age assignments? Perhaps some scientists ignore the evidence for recent creation not because it's unscientific, but because they are simply unwilling to admit they are wrong, or unwilling to face the idea that there really hasn't been enough time for evolution to have occurred. There are other reasons, but they are all poor excuses for excluding these many solid reasons for a recent creation.

Interpretation of radiometric age dating by many in the scientific community has drastically inflated the age of the Earth. Old radioisotope ages assigned to newly formed rocks diminishes those techniques' reliability as "age" indicators. If it cannot be trusted for young rocks, then how can it be trusted for ones that are supposedly old? Two minerals, zircon and diamonds, are about as close to a closed system as we can imagine. And yet, zircon crystals contain too much helium, and the atmosphere does not have enough to support the idea of an Earth that is billions or even millions of years old. Measurable amounts of carbon-14 in diamonds demonstrate that the Earth is only thousands of years old. Carbon-14 in coal of supposedly different ages indicates that the plant debris really lived in the same time period—what biblical creationists call the pre-Flood age. This is further demonstrated by the fact that the coals not only were sampled from different stratigraphic levels but also from widely separated locations. The consistency of the data and care with which they were acquired rule out contamination as an excuse for their young (relative to millions of years) carbon ages.

The carbon-14 ages of 40,000 to 65,000 years for coal seem to be very accurate and are much closer to the biblical age. But the Earth can even be younger than this. Fossils and fossil fuels demonstrate that the original Earth at the time of creation contained many more living things than today. The Flood and its aftereffects buried much of it. This large biomass—the total contribution of life to Earth's mass—is estimated to have been about 100 times greater than the total biosphere of living plants and animals today. This would have caused a much lower percent modern carbon (pMC) ratio of $^{14}C/C$, allowing us to reduce the calculated carbon ages to just several thousand years, which is more consistent with Scripture.[85]

This young age for the Earth matches quite well with the produced helium within the zircon crystals forming in about 6,000 years and the destruction of DNA within 10,000 years, which has even been found in dinosaur bones. These ages also match well with the recorded histories of mankind, the population growth rate of mankind which calculates to only a few thousand years, and the chronology in the Bible.

Chapter 4:

Do Fossils Show Evolution?

David V. Bassett, M.S.

Why is this Chapter Important?

There is no more fundamentally important debate raging in the midst of the current global culture war of ideas than the controversy over origins. The creation-evolution issue is foundational to everyone's worldview and, as such, is a priority topic that must be regarded, wrestled with, and ultimately resolved. Since ultimate origins are "one-time only" happenings of the unobservable, non-repeatable past (referred to as "singularities"), they must *philosophically be accepted by faith*, based on what one believes about the beginning history of the Universe, of the Earth, of life, and of mankind. These faith-beliefs, in turn, result in predictions about the present-day world of which we are a part. Consequently, these expectations can be either confounded or confirmed by observable evidence and/or scientific experimentation. This line of reasoning can, and should, be applied to the fossil record of the Earth's surface rocks since these layers are present-day evidence of past geological processes and their fossil contents are present-day evidence of past biological organisms. The fossil record is thus where one should look to find scientific answers about the Earth's early history and its ancient life forms.

If the reader were to objectively examine the testimony of Earth's surface rocks and the fossil remains contained therein for insight regarding origins, they would find that the fossil record does not uphold *any* textbook claim that the fossils document evolutionary progression and random change through only natural means over hundreds of millions of years. It is this atheistic *religion of naturalism* (aka evolutionary humanism) which is being continuously—sometimes forcefully—promoted by our culture in an all-out attempt to secularize our society away from the belief that the cosmos has been created by a supernatural, eternal Being to whom we are morally responsible and inevitably accountable since we have been created—not evolved!—in His image. It is only this latter, bible-based understanding (as revealed in the early chapters of the Book of Genesis) that is instead overwhelmingly confirmed by the fossil record's silent proclamation of detailed design, downward development and diversity, and the deluge-driven death of Noah's Flood!

In short, the fossils glaringly support the young-Earth biblical history of the recent, special creation of our world followed by a single Earth-covering Flood on our planet less than 4,400 years ago. Thus, accepting the faith-claims of evolutionary naturalism or secular humanism as the proper perspective for interpreting the physical world (as relentlessly encouraged by today's public educational system and, unfortunately, also increasingly so by the private-school sector as well) is to be indoctrinated into a never-settled, anti-evidence religious system that is neither justified by thoughtful, consistent reasoning nor verified by solid, scientific evidence.

Introduction

Most scientific hypotheses describe experimentally repeatable occurrences which are directly observable in the present. Charles Darwin's concept of "*phyletic gradualism*," the belief that all *phyla* (i.e., complex fundamental groups of living organisms) are biologically related to each other by means of *gradual*, upward evolution from a single-celled, ancestral form of the ancient past is, however, outside the scope of the scientific method of objective, observed, operational science.

By contrast, an explanatory framework, not a scientific hypothesis, deals with unique, irreversible, non-repeating, one-time-only events of the past—referred to as "ultimate origins" or "singularities." These fall in the realm of origin-science, also called forensic science. As first explained in the introduction to this book, origin-science hypotheses are open to both the individual opinion and worldview biases of the interpreter, and cannot be directly checked by the observation, theorization, and experimentation of the scientific method. Instead, their truth claims are evaluated by either comparing similarities between present and past causes or by considering circumstantial evidence through a pre-supposed, faith-based (biblical or naturalistic) worldview perspective.

Therefore, in the absence of direct observations made over supposed "deep time" (see introduction), Darwinists interpret the fossil record, or the remains of past life found within the rocks of the Earth's crust, as circumstantial evidence that biological species have originated solely by means of "natural selection" from a universal common ancestor. Do fossils really show the evolutionary "tree of life" preserved in stone? Thus, this Darwinian model that all life that has ever existed on Earth is one grand, biologically-related family would predict that this fossil record should show the following three features:

1. Ancestral Forms: Lowest rocks contain few relatively "simple" ancestral life forms (i.e., *the less-evolved root organisms*).

2. Intermediate Forms: Life forms gradually display new organs and other body designs in an uninterrupted, increasingly advanced chain (i.e., *the transitional trunk*).
3. Divergent Forms: Ever-increasing numbers of more and more genetically complex diverse organisms (i.e., *the more-evolved branches*) occupy the higher geological strata.

Upon closer inspection, however, the fossil record actually falsifies *all three* evolutionary model predictions. Instead, the fossil record biologically, paleontologically, and geologically supports *all* biblical creation criteria without exception. Each of these three will be evaluated next.

Strike One!—Evolutionary "Ancestral Forms" Never Existed

Rather than phyla coming about by natural selection, somehow adding new genes and organs to pre-existent ancestors as Darwin's ideas predicted, the fossil record provides no hint in the lowest known fossil-bearing rocks (named "Precambrian" and "Cambrian") of single-celled organisms morphing into the multi-celled creatures. The "Cambrian Explosion" describes the sudden appearance of all the radically-different blueprint types of each animal all in one rock system. This gap—which has been confirmed within the fossil record globally—should not even exist locally if evolutionism is true.

Jonathan Wells, in his eye-opening book entitled *Icons of Evolution: Science or Myth?— Why Much of What We Teach about Evolution Is Wrong* wrote:

> ...in Darwin's theory, there is no way phylum-level differences could have appeared right at the start.

> Yet that is what the fossil record shows... In other words, the highest levels of the biological hierarchy appeared right at the start. Darwin was aware of this, and considered it a major difficulty for his theory... Darwin was convinced, however, that the difficulty was only apparent.... Many paleontologists are now convinced that the major groups of animals really *did* appear abruptly in the early Cambrian. The fossil evidence is so strong, and the event so dramatic, that it has become known as "the Cambrian explosion," or "biology's big bang"[86] (emphasis added).

This sudden appearance of all the major, complex body-plans of biology in the lowest of the sedimentary rock layers without any clear-cut, "simpler" forms gradually leading up to them argues against evolution. This same evidence, however, can easily be interpreted as scientific support for the biblical teaching of an Earth-covering Flood rapidly burying the God-designed creatures of the pre-Flood ocean bottom at the very beginning of this catastrophe! Mr. Van Wingerden describes this Flood in Chapter 2.

Strike Two!—Evolutionary "Transitional Forms" Never Existed

If all living things are indeed related to each other through a gradual development of pre-existing organisms as Charles Darwin said, and as is often illustrated by so-called branching "evolutionary tree" diagrams known as "phylogenetic charts," then we would expect to find countless intermediate species or transitional forms (i.e., one animal kind turning into another) between major biological groupings like phyla. Transitional *creatures*, supposedly exemplified by such headliners as ape-to-man "hominids," the coelacanth fish,[87] and Archaeopteryx (an extinct bird that evolutionists believe possesses some reptilian-like features causing it to be classified as an evolutionary transitional form[88]) are supposed to bridge classification boundaries by possessing transitional *features*.

However, even Archaeopteryx—promoted by evolutionists at one time as the prime example of an intermediate form or "missing link" candidate between reptiles and birds—would not qualify as a *transitional* fossil since its socketed teeth, long bony tail, and wing-claws are all *fully-formed* structures of its alleged fossil representatives, showing no signs of *partial* evolutionary development. Without true transitional structures, does the fossil record support or upsettingly contradict the Darwinian view of phyletic gradualism? Percival Davis and Dean H. Kenyon ask in their book, *Of Pandas and People* (1989):

> Does Darwin's theory match the story told by the fossils? To find out, we must first ask, what kind of story would it match? His theory posited that living things formed a continuous chain back to one or a few original cells. If the theory is true, the fossils should show a continuous chain of creatures, each taxon leading smoothly to the next. In other words, there should be a vast number of transitional forms connecting each taxon with the one that follows. The differences separating major groups in taxonomy [such as invertebrates and the first fish] are so great that they must have been bridged by a huge number of transitional forms. As Darwin himself noted in *The Origin of Species* (1859), "The number of intermediate varieties, which formerly existed on earth [must] be truly enormous." *Yet this immense number of intermediates simply does not exist in the fossil record.* The fossils do not reveal a string of creatures leading up to fish, or to reptiles, or to birds. Darwin

> conceded this fact: "Why then is not every geological formation and every stratum full of such intermediate links? *Geology assuredly does not reveal any such finely graduated organic chain.*" Indeed, this is, in Darwin's own words, "the most obvious and gravest objection which can be urged against my theory"[89] (emphasis added).

If evolutionary gradualism were true, then every organism's genetics would be evolving out of its inferior/past/ancestral code into a superior/future/descendant form. In short, *every life-form would be transitional* between what it once was and what it is evolving into. However, the fossil record does not match this idea. The origin of every distinct, self-bounded biological body plan is not connected by evolutionary intermediates with transitioning structures at all, either to the supposed "universal common ancestor" or to the plentiful variety within its own bounded phylum!

Instead, all preserved and present phyla demonstrate *stasis*—the dominant fossil trend of maintaining anatomical sameness. They show essentially no change in appearance over time, though some show a decrease in size. In addition, 95% of the fossil record phyla are comprised of marine invertebrates, some of which are found throughout its entire vertical span of rocks.[90] Thus, the completeness of the fossil record is being finally recognized after more than 150 years of fossil collecting and more than 200,000,000 fossils found. *Newsweek*'s 1980 admission of Darwin's elusive intermediate species being only imaginative is still embarrassingly accurate:

> The missing link between man and apes... is merely the most glamorous of a whole hierarchy of phantom creatures. *In the fossil record, missing links are the rule*... The more scientists have searched for the

> transitional forms between species, the more they have been frustrated.[91] (emphasis added)

In their journal disclosure, evolutionists Stephen Jay Gould and Niles Eldridge have honestly admitted the pseudo-scientific, philosophical origin of Darwin's view by their candid confession that *"Phyletic gradualism* [gradual evolution]... *was never 'seen' in the rocks* ... It [gradualism] expressed the cultural and political biases of 19th century liberalism" (emphasis added).[92] Thus, the "onward and upward" notion of evolutionary progress involving innovation and integration was a product of various social prejudices, not science.

Darwin had every hope that future research would reveal numerous transitional forms in the fossil record.[93] Now, after 150+ years of digging and millions of additional fossils identified and catalogued, do we have enough evidence to conclude whether transitional forms exist? Remember, if evolution is true, it would take numerous "prior versions" to move between forms—e.g., from a mouse to a bat.

To investigate this issue, Dr. Carl Werner and his wife Debbie invested over 14 years of their lives investigating "the best museums and dig sites around the globe [and] photographing thousands of original fossils and the actual fossil layers where they were found."[94]

After visiting hundreds of museums and interviewing hundreds of paleontologists, scientists, and museum curators, Dr. Werner concluded: "Now, 150 years after Darwin wrote his book, this problem still persists. Overall, the fossil record is rich—200 million fossils in museums—but the predicted evolutionary ancestors are missing, seemingly contradicting evolution."[95] He continues with a series of examples:

- Museums have collected the fossil remains of 100,000 individual dinosaurs, but have not found a single direct ancestor for any dinosaur species.

- Approximately 200,000 fossil birds have been found, but ancestors of the oldest birds have yet to be discovered.
- The remains of 100,000 fossilized turtles have been collected by museums, yet the direct ancestors of turtles are missing.
- Nearly 1,000 flying reptiles (pterosaurs) have been collected, but no ancestors showing ground reptiles evolving into flying reptiles have been found.
- Over 1,000 fossil bats have been collected by museums, but no ancestors have been found showing a ground mammal slowly evolving into a flying mammal.
- Approximately 500,000 fossil fish have been collected, and 100,000,000 invertebrates have been collected, but ancestors for the theoretical first fish—a series of fossils showing an invertebrate changing into a fish—are unknown.
- Over 1,000 fossil sea lions have been collected, but not a single ancestor of sea lions has been found.
- Nearly 5,000 fossilized seals have been collected, but not a single ancestor has been found.

If this was not enough, one more key consideration should clearly convince. What if, after countless millions of hours spent by researchers mining the crust of the Earth for fossil evidence, the fossil record is essentially *complete*? That is, it stands to reason that the millions of fossils we have collected over the last 150 years *exhaustively* record all basic life forms that ever lived, with only a few additional "big surprises" to be found. Given this, can we say that the question of transitional forms has been *asked and answered*?

One way to find out is to "calculate the percentage of those animals living today that have also been found as fossils. In other words, if the fossil record is comprised of a high percentage of animals that are living today, then the fossil record could be viewed as being fairly complete; that is, most animals that have lived on the Earth have been fossilized and discovered."[96] Carl Werner provides a chart demonstrating the results of such an investigation:[97]

- Of the 43 living land animal *orders*, such as carnivores, rodents, bats, and apes, nearly all, or 97.7% have been found as fossils. This means that at least one example from each animal order has been collected as a fossil.
- Of the 178 living land animal *families*, such as dogs, bears, hyenas, and cats, 87.8% have been found in fossils.

Evolution has had its chance—over 150 years and millions of fossils—to prove itself, and it has come up wanting. The theory has been weighed, tested, measured, and falsified. Aren't 200 million opportunities and one and one-half centuries enough time to answer the issue that *confounded* Darwin himself?

> Why, if species have descended from other species by fine gradations, do we not everywhere see innumerable transitional forms? Why is not all nature in confusion, instead of the species being, as we see them, well defined?...But, as by this theory innumerable transitional forms must have existed, why do we not find them embedded in countless numbers in the crust of the earth?...But in the intermediate region, having intermediate conditions of life, why do we not now find closely-linking intermediate varieties? This difficulty for a long time quite confounded me. [98]

Strike Three!—Evolutionary "Divergent Forms" Never Existed

Darwinian evolution predicts that as phyla continue to diverge or branch out from their ancestral, evolutionary stock, their numbers should increase just as tree limbs radiate from a central trunk and then multiply outward from each other. According to Wells, "Some biologists have described this in terms of 'bottom-up' versus 'top-down' evolution. *Darwinian evolution is 'bottom-up,' referring to its prediction that lower levels in the biological hierarchy should emerge before higher ones. But the Cambrian explosion shows the opposite*" (emphasis added).[99] The fossil record evidence indicates that the number of phyla in fact decreases from about 50–60 at the "Cambrian Explosion" to approximately 37 living phyla. Extinction—the opposite of evolution's required new phyla—have certainly occurred.[100] *"Clearly the Cambrian fossil record explosion is not what one would expect from Darwin's theory.* Since higher levels of the biological hierarchy appear first, one could even say that the Cambrian explosion stands Darwin's tree of life on its head" (emphasis added).[101]

Rather than a "bottom-up" continuum of ever-morphing divergent forms, the fossil record clearly reveals definite gaps between, and "top-down" hierarchical variation within, phyla. In fact, these anatomical differences separating major design themes make biological classification of organisms (taxonomy) possible![102] Without these clear-cut gaps between organism kinds, biologists would not be able to divide plants and animals into their respective kingdoms, phyla, classes, orders, families, genera, and species.

Those familiar with the Bible will recognize that one would expect these gaps between biological kinds if all terrestrial life reproduced "after its own kind," a truth that the Scriptures declares *ten times* in its first chapter (Genesis 1:11,

12, 21, 24, 25). In fact, even the New Testament affirms that "All flesh is not the same flesh, but there is one kind of flesh of men, another flesh of beasts, another of fish, and another of birds" (1 Corinthians 15:39). Obviously, since God's written Word lists different creature groupings as separate kinds with anatomically unique "flesh," biological classification ultimately describes "a created arboretum" of various types of trees, and not a single "evolutionary tree of life" that connects all organisms as Charles Darwin proposed.

With No Fossil Evidence to Support It, Gradualism Strikes Out!

Those who have scientifically examined the fossil record firsthand are justifiably adamant that it completely falsifies all three of the essential evolutionary elements needed to substantiate the concept of an integrated "tree of life." The fossil record bears witness that there are (1) *no ancestral roots*—no "primitive" organisms between microfossils and visible life, (2) *no transitional trunk*—no anatomically-intermediate creatures with structurally-transitional features (e.g., partially-evolved organs, limbs, etc.), and (3) *no divergent branches*—no new phyla being genetically descended from less-evolved "common ancestors."

Explaining the Fossil Record—A Creation Model Homerun!

Well, if the fossil record does not support the evolutionary predictions of ancestral roots, transitional trunk, and divergent branches with regard to the major categories of life, what does it show? To summarize thus far, the fossil record clearly reveals the following about the major classification divisions of organisms:

1. Separation from other phyla by definite, unbridgeable gaps with no ancestor-descendant/bottom-to-top transitional-relationship;
2. All forms suddenly appear as unique body plans with fully-formed characteristic structures;
3. All phyla are represented from the beginning by fossil forms, thus demonstrating fossil-record completeness;
4. All are complex, functional, and were or still are able to survive;
5. All show no innovative change in their basic anatomical form after they first appear as fossils—only minor, top-down variation within a blueprint design;
6. Nearly all (95%) are phyla of marine invertebrates;
7. Many of these are found throughout the fossil record, not restricted to a certain vertical range of rock; and
8. Extinction has decreased the number of sub-kingdom plant and animal classification divisions from 50–60 phyla to nearly 37 phyla—the opposite direction of evolution.

In addition, the fossil record confirms biblical creation/global Flood predictions by showing the following:

9. Polystrate fossils cutting across multiple rock layers, supporting rapid sedimentation and catastrophic burial of life-forms;
10. Fossil graveyard deposits;
11. Mass killing and the violent death of creatures;
12. Mixed groupings of organisms from various ecological zones of different habitat and elevation;
13. Highly energetic, destructive processes capable of burying organisms alive, ripping creatures apart, and/or transporting their carcasses great distances;

14. Rock formations with mostly ocean-dwelling creatures catastrophically fossilized;
15. All fossils in continental rocks, not ocean-bottom sediments;
16. Some geologic deposits covering hundreds of thousands of square miles and spanning several continents.

With this being the case, it should therefore be quite obvious that the fossil record is not at all like Charles Darwin's interpretation of an evolutionary "tree of life" preserved in stone. The fossil record has indeed had the last word!

Chapter 5:

Do Fossils of Early Man Prove Evolution?

David V. Bassett, M.S.

Why is this Chapter Important?

The pursuit of paleoanthropology (the study of ancient man) is by its very nature an area of heated debate and fierce controversy. This is partly because its subject matter involves biased interpretations of fossil evidence regarding the origin and livelihood of mankind's ancestors from warring worldview perspectives. More so, however, paleoanthropology generates such deep emotion due to the fact that these contrasting philosophical interpretations of the same scientific evidence both seek to define the core essence of what it means to be human. Are we temporarily "a little lower than the angels" (Psalm 8:5) or is man merely "a little higher than the apes"?

The evolutionary bias would answer the fundamental questions of philosophy: (1) "Who am I?" (Identity), (2) "Where did I come from?" (Origins), (3) "Why am I here?" (Purpose), and (4) "Where am I going?" (Destiny) with the following typical textbook conclusions: (1) We are nothing more than the arbitrary, random product of time, chance, and natural forces, (2) that ultimately came from nothing through lifeless chemicals through primordial protoplasm through hundreds of millions of years of meandering, amoeba-to-ape ancestry, (3) with our life-purpose only being to pass our "DNA baton" to the next generation, and (4) our death-destiny being solely to enrich the soil and feed bacteria as we rot with worms. Talk about Darwin's "descent of man"!

The opposing creationary bias (based on God's written Word, the Bible), however, instead teaches that (1 & 2) the first man and woman were the climax creation of a good and all-powerful Creator in Whose image they were patterned less than 6,200 years ago. Our first parents were not only a unique kind (i.e., *man*kind)—not at all related to the animals—but they, like each of us, were also unique among their/our own kind. (3) This Creator-God loved mankind so much that He made a way for us to spend eternity with Him (John 3:16). This way—*The* Way (John 14:6)—is to accept Jesus Christ (God in the flesh) as our personal Savior to rescue us from sin's ultimate penalty—eternal separation from this holy God. Our purpose—to be in a covenant relationship with our Creator—is summarized in Micah 6:8 as to "do justly, and to love mercy, and to walk humbly with thy God" and in Ecclesiastes 12:13 as "Fear God, and keep His commandments; for this is the whole duty of man." (4) Our ideal destiny is, therefore, to live forever in Christ's kingdom and to reign with Him over the universe.

Thus, what one believes about paleoanthropology does have profound implications with everlasting consequences. The fossil evidence, when examined closely, clearly shows that apes have always been apes and man has always been man, just as the Bible says!

Introduction

The origin of humanity, without question, has always been the most controversial aspect of the "molecule-to-man" evolutionary myth. In 1871, Charles Darwin claimed in his book *The Descent of Man* that mankind gradually evolved upward from a specie(s) of Old World monkey. However, Paul S. Taylor objectively conveys the current evolutionary position in the following statement with the insight that the only "evolution" that has taken place is of Darwin's proposal and of evolution itself:

> Museums and textbooks controlled by believers in Evolutionism have frequently taught that there is abundant evidence that man and ape have evolved from common ancestors. The public is shown imaginative pictures which claim to depict how man's ancestors looked and behaved. But what are the facts? Did the human beings evolve? *The safest analysis of the evidence seems to indicate all the fossils involved are either of extinct apes—or humans—or hoaxes* (emphasis added).[103]

Indeed, most of the fossils that supposedly prove man's alleged animal ancestry clearly fit one of these general categories, with none of them undisputedly fitting any "transitional" category:

1. "Misidentified Mammal,"
2. "Wholly Human," or
3. "Deliberate Deception."[104]

Let us take a closer look at two of the evolutionist's prime examples from each of these categories.

Misidentified Mammal

Nebraska Man (Hesperopithecus harlodcookii: "Harold Cook's Western Ape")

Ardent evolutionary paleontologist Henry Fairfield Osborn, then head of the American Museum of Natural History, proclaimed in 1922 that a single molar tooth, found by geologist Harold J. Cook in 1917, to have belonged to the first pithecanthropoid (ape-man) of the Americas, hence the name "western ape." Meanwhile, in England, the British evolutionist Grafton Elliot Smith was afterward knighted for his efforts in publicizing "Nebraska Man" in the globally-distributed *Illustrated London News*. There, he printed an imaginative "reconstruction" of the tooth's owner as an erect, naked, club-carrying ape-man with tools, possibly domesticated animals, and a brutish bride (gathering roots, no less)—all derived from the artistic inspiration from this single tooth!

In July 1925, this selfsame lone molar was to be the prime, pro-evolution evidence against creationism in the so-called Scopes "Monkey Trial" held in Dayton, Tennessee. However, excavations in 1927–1928 at Cook's Nebraska riverbed site revealed that the tooth belonged to *neither hominid* (man or "man-like ape") *or pongid* (true ape*), but of an extinct peccary—a wild pig*! Back then it was named *Prosthennops serus*, but is now named *Catagonus wagneri*. Its false identity was used to propagate human evolution.[105] Then, in 1972, living herds of this same pig were discovered in Paraguay, South America, and named *Catagonus ameghino*.[106] According to the late renowned creation scientist Duane T. Gish, "this is a case in which a scientist made a man out of a pig, and then the pig made a monkey out of the scientist!"[107]

Australopithecus afarensis ("Southern Ape from the Afar Triangle of Ethiopia"): "Lucy"

Evolutionists claimed Lucy to be descended from *Ramapithecus*—now recognized as resembling an Ethiopian baboon *Theropithecus gelada*—between 3 and 4 million years ago. They promoted Lucy as our oldest-known direct ancestor, and named it after the Beatles' song *Lucy in the Sky with Diamonds,* which was playing in the base camp at the time of "her" discovery. *Lucy,* or *Australopithecus afarensis*, is the most popularized of the australopithecine fossils. Unearthed by a team led by Donald C. Johanson at Hadar (Ethiopia) in 1974–1975, Lucy was a 40% complete skeleton some 3-1/2 to 4 feet tall that did not include most of the skull, the upper jaw, nor hand and foot bones.

The skeletal evidence that was present, however, seemed to indicate a "real swinger… based on anatomical data, *A. afarensis* must have been arboreal [tree-dwelling]…Lucy's pelvis shows a flare that is better suited for climbing than for walking."[108] Later-discovered specimens of *A. afarensis* exhibited both the long curved fingers and toes of tree-dwellers, as well as the restricted wrist anatomy of knuckle-walking gorillas and chimps—anatomy that keeps them from being able to manipulate tools like the uniquely human hand can.[109] Sir Solly Zuckerman, chief scientific advisor to the British government, has emphatically stated regarding the cranium (braincase), "The australopithecine skull is in fact so overwhelmingly simian (ape-like), as opposed to human that the contrary position could be equated to an assertion that black is white."[110]

In fact, Wray Herbert admits that his fellow paleo-anthropologist Adrienne "Zihlman compares the pygmy chimpanzee (*Pan paniscus*) to "Lucy," one of the oldest hominid fossils known, and finds the similarities striking. They are almost identical in body size, in stature and in brain size."[111] Indeed, according to Albert W. Mehlert "the evidence... makes it overwhelmingly likely that *Lucy was no more than a variety of pygmy chimpanzee,* and walked the same way (awkwardly upright on occasions, but mostly quadrupedal). The 'evidence' for the alleged transformation from ape to man is extremely unconvincing"[112] (emphasis added). Creation researcher and author of the book *Bones of Contention* Marvin Lubenow rightly wrote:

> ... there are no fossils of *Australopithecus* or of any other primate stock in the proper time period to serve as evolutionary ancestors to humans. *As far as we can tell from the fossil record, when humans first appear in the fossil record they are already human.*[113] (emphasis added)

DeWitt Steele and Gregory Parker succinctly conclude, therefore, that "*A. afarensis can probably be dismissed as a type of extinct chimpanzee*"[114] (emphasis added). Last, Lucy-like fossils occur within the same-dated strata as human fossils. If they lived at the same time, then one could not have evolved into the other. Textbook claims and museum displays of Lucy walking on human feet subject fossil and anatomical evidence to evolutionary wishful thinking. Lucy as a human ancestor has been misplaced, since it was actually just an extinct kind of ape.

Ardipithecus ramidus ("Ground/floor" "Monkey" "Root"): "Ardi"

Nick-named "Ardi" for short, this fossil was first discovered in the early 1990s and is hailed by some as another evolutionary link to humans. Because Ardi's remains were so badly damaged, it took 15 years to reconstruct what is now still only a very incomplete fossil that is said to be 4.4

million years old.[115] The first 17 bone fragments (including skull, mandible, teeth, and arm bones) were discovered in 1992 and more fragments were recovered in 1994. When combined, these fragments represent *only 45% of the total skeleton*. Ardi's brain size is estimated to be only about 350 ccs—about the same size of a modern chimp, and much smaller than the average human brain, which is about 1330 ccs.[116]

Brian Thomas, science writer for the Institute for Creation Research (ICR.org) remarks that Ardi was distinctly ape-like:

> She had hands for feet, and the long, curved bones of her fingers and toes clearly show that Ardi was adept at living in trees. The Ardipithecus foot has its big toe "thumb" projecting strikingly sideways, which is hardly human-like. Nor are its other foot bones like those of chimps and gorillas, which have specially flexible feet that enable them to climb vertical tree trunks. Ardi's feet are like those of some of today's monkeys, which have a stable platform from which to leap, along with a fully developed grasping structure.[117]

If evolution is true, one would expect *countless millions of transitions* from ape-like creatures leading to the incredible human design that we have today. Instead, all the fossil record presents are these occasional ape-like creatures that are only imagined to line-up progressively to humans.

Darwinius masillae: "Ida"

When Ida was first found in 1983, news reports hailed her as "the eighth wonder of the world," "the Holy Grail," and "a Rosetta Stone." Interestingly, this dogmatic hype concerning Ida in the May 2009 headlines was quietly rescinded just three months later (in August of 2009) when scientists admitted that Ida was nothing more than an extinct variety of lemur.[118] This cat-sized primate fossil (that supposedly lived 47 million years ago) continued to be met with great uncertainty in the scientific community, mostly due to Ida's quite obvious lemur-like features, including "grasping hands, opposable thumbs, clawless digits with nails, and relatively short limbs."[119]

Viewing this fossil through a "Creationist lens" leads to the following observations and conclusions:

1. Nothing about this fossil suggests it is anything other than an extinct, lemur-like creature. Its appearance is far from chimpanzee, let alone "ape-man" or human.
2. [In general] A fossil can never show evolution. Fossils are unchanging records of dead organisms. Evolution is an alleged process of change in live organisms. Fossils show "evolution" only if one presupposes evolution, then uses that presupposed belief to interpret the fossil. Circular reasoning at its best . . . or worst!
3. Similarities can never show evolution. If two organisms have similar structures, the only thing it proves is that the two have similar structures. One must presuppose evolution to say that the similarities are due to evolution rather than design. Furthermore, when it comes to "transitional forms," the slightest similarities often receive great attention while major differences are ignored.
4. The remarkable preservation is a hallmark of rapid burial. Team member Jørn Hurum of the University of Oslo said, "This fossil is so complete. Everything's there. It's unheard of in the primate record at all. You have to get to human burial to see something that's this complete." Even the contents of Ida's stomach were preserved. While the researchers believe Ida

sunk to the bottom of a lake and was buried, this preservation is more consistent with a catastrophic flood. Yet Ida was found with "hundreds of well-preserved specimens."

5. If evolution were true, there would be real transitional forms. Instead, the best "missing links" evolutionists can come up with are strikingly similar to organisms we see today, usually with the exception of minor, controversial, and inferred anatomical differences.
6. Evolutionists only open up about the lack of fossil missing links once a new one is found. *Sky News* reports, "Researchers say proof of this transitional species finally confirms Charles Darwin's theory of evolution," while Attenborough commented that the missing link "is no longer missing." So are they admitting the evidence was missing until now (supposedly)?[120]

It seems to take a giant leap of faith to believe that such 47-million year lemurs can evolve into modern-day humans. Doesn't it take *less faith* to believe that this creature was simply a lemur-like animal that was created on Day 6 of Creation Week?

Wholly Human

Neandert(h)al Man

Neandertal man was named after the Neander Valley near Dusseldorf in west Germany where the first fossils were found in 1856; so called due to the frequent visits there by hymn writer Joachem Neander + *tal*, or *thal* in Old German, meaning "valley." From true man to "missing link" to variant form of modern human, the taxonomic history of the Neandertals is as interesting as the people themselves.

Originally, "when the first Neandertal was discovered in 1856, even "Darwin's bulldog," Thomas Henry Huxley, recognized that it was fully human and not an evolutionary ancestor."[121] Nevertheless, the evolutionary bias of anatomist William King reinterpreted them as a separate, primitive species of man (*Homo neanderthalensis*), where they remained taxonomically until 1964. Today, with more than 200 known specimens representing 40+ discovery sites in Europe, Asia, and Africa, "Neandethal fossils are the most plentiful in the world (of paleoanthropology)."[122] This mound of data has testified in recent decades to the fact that, "while the Neandertals may not have been as culturally sophisticated as the people who followed, . . . the Neandertal people were not primitive but the *most highly specialized* of all the humans of the past" [123] (emphasis added). "Evolutionists now admit that the Neanderthals were 100% human; they are classified as *Homo sapiens neanderthalensis*, designating them as a (subspecies) variety of modern humans."[124] Their skeletons reveal them to have been superior to modern man both in brawn (being up to 30% larger in body mass) and brains (with a more than 13% larger cranial capacity—nearly 200cc more brain volume)!

However, "the strongest evidence that Neanderthals were fully human and of our species is that, at four sites [3 in Israel and 1 in Croatia], Neandertals and modern humans were buried together," indicating that "they lived together, worked together, intermarried, and were accepted as members of the same family, clan, and community" since generational "reproduction is on the species level."[125] Neandertal burials include jewelry and purses, showing they had nothing to do with any ape-kind. Strikingly, the Neandertal burial practice of using caves as family burial grounds or tribal cemeteries exactly parallels that of the post-Babel patriarchs of Genesis, for example Abraham (Genesis 23:17–20), Isaac (Genesis 25:7–11), and Jacob (Genesis 49:29–32.)

The longevity of the Neandertal people also looks astonishingly similar to the lifespan of those living in the post-Flood generations including Peleg (Genesis. 11:12–17). Using recent dental studies and digitized x-rays, computer-generated projections of orthodontic patients have illustrated the continuing growth of their craniofacial bones. These show a Neandertal-like profile of the skull as the patient advances into their 300th, 400th, 500th year of simulated life.[126] Dr. Cuozzo's analysis of the teeth and jaw development in children, and "studies on aging reveal that the older we get, the more our faces begin to look like those of Neanderthal man. And the most accurate assumption that can be made about these strange-looking skeletons that are not old enough to be fossilized is that they have been alive long enough for their bones to change into those shapes—they are skeletons of patriarchs who lived hundreds of years, but have only been dead for thousands of years, not millions!"[127]

Creation researchers have been saying for decades that Neandertal man was wholly human, with no hint of a single evolutionary transitional feature. Neandertal DNA sequences published in 2010 confirmed this, showing that certain of today's people groups share bits of Neandertal-specific DNA sequences.[128]

Cro-Magnon Man

Cro-Magnon Man is known as the "big hole man" in the French dialect local to the initial 1868 discovery site, a cave in the Dordogne area of Les Eyzies in the southwest SW France. Once regarded as our most recent evolutionary ancestors on the "ape-to-man" hominid family tree, "evolutionists now admit that Cro-Magnons were modern humans. Cro-Magnons are classified as *Homo sapiens sapiens* ['wise, wise man'], the same classification assigned humans today."[129] Creation writer Vance Ferrell echoes this consensus with his assessment that "the Cro-Magnons were *normal people*, *not monkeys*; and they provide no evidence of a transition from ape to man"[130] (emphasis added). With interests ranging from mundane, stone tools, fishhooks, and spears to more sublime activities like astronomy, art, and the afterlife, "every kind of evidence that we have a right to expect from the fossil and archeological record indicates that the Cro-Magnon and Neandertal peoples were *humans in the same ways that we are human*."[131]

Contrary to popular belief, Cro-Magnon use of caves gives every indication of being only for ritualistic, not residential, purposes. In addition, authenticated etchings on the cave walls at Minetada, Spain (1915), and La Marche, central France (1937), depict Cro-Magnon men with clipped and groomed beards while the women display dresses and elegant hair styles.[132] Advanced not only in manner but also in morphology, "the Cro-Magnons were truly human, possibly of a noble bearing. Some were over six feet tall, with a cranial volume somewhat larger (by 200cc–400cc) than that of man today."[133] Brain size should not be exclusively used to judge whether or not a given specimen was human or not, but it can, in combination with other skull features, add its testimony. In any case, just as with Neandertal man, Cro Magnon men were men—wholly human.

Deliberate Deception

Java Man (Pithecanthropus erectus: "Erect Ape-man")

"Java Man" is based on a small collection of bones found on the Indonesian island of Java by Dutch anatomist and physician Eugene DuBois in 1891. They consisted of a skullcap that looked similar to that of a large ape and three teeth. One tooth was later determined to be human, and the other two teeth to be those of an orangutan. Nearly 150 feet away and a year later, he also discovered a femur, or thighbone, that later studies showed matched totally human femurs. Some believe the skullcap to potentially indicate a near-human cranial capacity, and have now chosen to classify Java Man as *Homo erectus—now recognized as 100% human*—along with so-called Peking Man (*Sinanthropus pekinensis* = "Chinese man from Peking"), though others believe this to be both unwarranted and undeserved, including Marvin Lubenow, who wrote:

> The Java Man skullcap and femur are evidence that the distinction between *Homo erectus* and *Homo sapiens* is an artificial one, that these two forms *are both truly human, and that they lived as contemporaries* [at the same time]. *The differences attributed to evolution are instead evidence of the wide genetic variation found in the human family.*[134] (emphasis added)

Interestingly, two definitely human skulls (called the Wadjak skulls) were found by DuBois in strata at the same level as the "Java Man" fossils—a fact which he kept secret for 30 years so that Java Man would be accepted as "the real missing link" by the international scientific community. Near the end of his life, however, DuBois publicly conceded that "Java Man" was extremely similar to—though he believed not identical with—a large gibbon. He himself wrote that "Pithecanthropus was not a man, but a gigantic genus allied to the Gibbons."[135] Scientific integrity took a back seat to other motives when "Java Man" had its heyday, helping evolutionists convince several generations that man evolved from ape-like ancestors. The real evidence simply shows that some people and some apes were fossilized, as distinct kinds, with no common ancestor.

Piltdown Man (Eoanthropus dawsoni: "Dawson's Dawn Man")

"Piltdown Man" is a fraudulent composite of fossil human skull fragments and a modern ape jaw with two teeth "discovered" by amateur antiquarian (collector of old things) Charles Dawson in a gravel pit at Piltdown, east Sussex, England. History testifies, as summarized by Pat Shipman, that "the Piltdown fossils, whose discovery was first announced in 1912, fooled many of the greatest minds in paleoanthropology until 1953, when the remains were revealed as planted, altered—a forgery."[136] Consider also the following deliberate (and desperate) measures some have gone to promote their faith in evolution:

> Piltdown Common had been used as a mass grave during the great plagues of A.D. 1348–9. The skull bones were quite thick, a characteristic of more ancient fossils, and *the skull had been treated with potassium bichromate* by Dawson to harden and preserve it... The other bones and stone tools had undoubtedly been planted in the pit and had been treated to match the dark brown color of the skull. *The lower jaw was that of a juvenile female orang-utan. The place where the jaw would articulate with the skull had been broken off to hide the fact that it did not fit the skull.* The teeth of the mandible [lower jaw] were filed down to match the teeth of the upper jaw, and the canine tooth had been filed down to make it look heavily worn... The amazing thing about the Piltdown hoax is that at least twelve different people have been accused of perpetrating the fraud... what has been called *the most successful scientific hoax of all time*.[137] (emphasis added)

In closing, consider Marvin Lubenow's conclusion after researching the ape and human fossil record literature for over 25 years:

> ... the evidence is strongly in favor of a morphological [rather than an evolutionary] continuum, both horizontally across species and vertically over time. The horizontal continuum shows that *anatomically modern Homo sapiens, Neandertal, archaic Homo sapiens, and Homo erectus all lived as contemporaries over extended periods of time*. The vertical continuum shows that as far back as the human fossil record goes *the human body has remained substantially the same and has not evolved from something else. This condition is what the creation model would predict. It is what we would expect if creation were true... new fossil discoveries have only strengthened the creationist position.*[138] (emphasis added)

Why do scientists continue to insist that man evolved from animals when no undisputed or convincing evidence aligns with this philosophy? None of the so-called "ape-man" fossils fit into any evolutionary progression; instead, they were either apes (extinct ape kinds, or modern-looking), wholly human, or tied to deception.

Chapter 6:

Natural Selection and Evolution: Do Darwin's Finches Prove Evolution?

Roger Patterson

Why is this Chapter Important?

As you open the typical biology textbook, you will be confronted with an evolutionary view of the world on almost every page. "Evolutionary processes" supposedly turn a single cell floating in an imaginary primordial ooze into a zebra fish or a zebra, and require billions of years to do so. Without these billions of years, natural selection and mutations would not have enough time to "work together" to bring about wholesale creature design changes—assuming they could do that even given an eternity. To accept the evolutionary development of life is to reject the clear meaning of God's description of the creation of life in Genesis 1. In this chapter you will learn of the differences between what evolutionists claim time and chance can accomplish and what we really know to be true from actual scientific studies and the description of God's creative acts in the Bible. Contrary to textbook assertions, you and I are far more than highly evolved animals, but special creations of God made in His image.

If you were to ask the typical person to explain biological evolution, the ideas of natural selection and mutations would surely be a part of their description. But is natural selection really able to accomplish what evolution needs it to accomplish? Can mutations account for the change of an amoeba into a horse? Has any of this actually been observed, or is there a lot of speculation involved? These are the kinds of questions that need to be answered as we sort through the claims found in textbooks and various video programs designed to teach the evolutionary view of how life came to exist on this planet.

The Naturalistic Worldview

Whenever we consider complex ideas like biological evolution, there are many assumptions that have to be made, or at least accepted, for the sake of discussion. The typical person who believes in an evolutionary process embraces a chain of assumptions—whether they realize it or not.

The explanations you will find in textbooks, various teaching videos, and hear in the classroom are almost always based on the worldview called naturalism. Those with a naturalistic worldview believe that everything we see in the universe can be explained by natural processes. To them, everything is a result of the laws of nature acting over time to produce what we see. Humans are simply the result of gravity, time, thermodynamics, natural selection, mutations, and chemical reactions. To a naturalist, there is no need for miracles or a god or anything we can't see and measure to produce the universe as we see it today—including every creature alive or extinct. In fact, the textbook you use might just include a statement like that in the early chapters that talk about what science is. In truth, we must assume uniformity of natural laws in order to achieve scientific discoveries about how things work. However, we must not assume that natural laws are all that ever existed, for, as discussed in the introduction, those very laws had their origin in a God entirely apart from nature.

A famous evolutionist, Dr. Richard Dawkins, admits that there are many elements of the natural world that look like they were designed. But he rejects the idea that there was a designer. Dawkins has said, "The illusion of purpose is so powerful that biologists themselves use the assumption of good design as a working tool"[139] and many other similar statements. When was the last time you saw a building or a watch and thought, "You know, I bet that just happened as a result of the random interactions of various natural laws?" Never. Take a look at your hand and flex your fingers. Move your eyes quickly around the room and consider how fast your eyes focus and take in new information. Next consider your hearing, and how air impulses from sound waves are converted into electrical impulses by your brain then interpreted as speech, almost in "real time." Now consider your whole body working together. Could an engineer design such an intricate machine? And could even the best of human engineers build it to repair and reproduce itself? Not a chance.

God has designed each of the kinds of living things that live on this planet. They did not arise from random events and natural laws. In order for those laws of nature to exist, there must have been a supreme Lawmaker, and He has told us in the Bible how He made all creatures. These creatures were not accidents. God purposefully designed each one in a supernatural act of creation. Every kind of creature was created by the powerful command of Jesus Christ (John 1:3; Colossians 1:16–17). Naturalism cannot offer a satisfactory explanation for how even a single-celled bacterium could have arrived on this planet without a designer. After all, the very laws of nature, such as diffusion and decay, tear away at life. Only the high-tech, ultraminiaturized programs and tools within living cells constantly battle against diffusion, decay, and other life-unfriendly "natural" laws.

Formula for Life

If evolution could be written as a formula, its simplest form would be Natural Selection + Mutations (changed to the genetic code) + Time = Evolution. But let's examine this idea a bit more carefully. For evolution to be a valid scientific theory, it has to be able to explain how the first life reproduced with variety so that future generations would be able to change into new kinds of organisms. Supposedly a bacterium changed into an amoeba, which changed into a sponge, which changed into a fish, which changed into a reptile, which changed into a human—and every other life form we see today. How scientific is this fantastic story?

All life has information inside of it encoded in its DNA. The DNA contains the genetic building and maintenance instructions for all of the parts of an organism. Plants can't make ears (other than corn!) because they don't have the right sequence of DNA instruction to produce ears. So if animals and plants have some common ancestor, at some point the information to make ears had to be added to the genes of some animal. So how did that extra information get there?

In order to exclude God from their thinking, most evolutionists must assume that information initially comes from a natural process in the first place. Otherwise, the first living cell would never have been able to make itself, let alone duplicate itself, without a miracle. This is one of the major hurdles in the hypothesis of chemical evolution—the origin of the first life. But let's assume that information in the DNA was present. If the DNA of an imaginary first organism was simply copied, evolution couldn't move forward in gaining new instructions because no differences would arise in future generations. The gene pool—all of the available genes in a population—would be stagnant.

Mutations

Enter mutations! If there were occasional mistakes in copying the information in the DNA, then differences could arise in future generations. The gene pool would have variety and slightly different organisms could be produced. Another way to introduce variety into the gene pool is through sexual reproduction, where each parent contributes half of the genetic information in its offspring, with different coding combinations possible. However, these processes occur according to very specific cellular and whole organism instructions. Where did those precise instructions come from?

DNA is made up of two molecular chains loosely bonded together. Each chain has a specific sequence of four chemical bases that pair up in specific ways. Adenine always bonds to Thymine, and Guanine always bonds to Cytosine. The DNA sequence is often represented by a series of As, Ts, Cs, and Gs. A particular strand of DNA might have the sequence ATTCGCATAATGAACCGTC. The sequence of letters serves as a template to produce proteins and other cellular products. The code is read in sets of three: ATT.CGC.ATA.ATG.AAC. GTC in the string above. If one of the letters is incorrectly copied when a cell is reproducing itself, the new cell gains a "point mutation." Other forms of mutations can involve letters being inserted into the code or sections of the code being deleted. In each of these cases, the mutation can cause the cell to die or it may not have any immediate impact at all.

Mutations are a measurable, observable process in cells—part of observational science. Understanding how a mutation impacts a given cell is an important part of biology and has helped us understand many diseases. Mutations resemble copying errors, like when we miss a letter or punctuation mark when we copy instructions from our teacher's marker board. An evolutionist takes these observable changes in cell's coding and tries to use them to explain how a bacterium could have changed into a bullfrog. This "origins exercise" involves assumptions. Evolutionary scientists try to make careful studies and perform experiments, but they start from the wrong place. They assume all life evolved from a single ancestor and then test their ideas to see if they are reasonable. In many cases, the explanations seem to make sense, but they leave God out of the picture and further investigation reveals how they violate scientific principles. Other chapters in this book give examples, revealing exciting discoveries that totally debunk evolutionary assertions that once sounded reasonable.

If we start from the Bible, we better understand why mutations do not add the coded instructions for life that evolution requires. Mutations are actually a product of the Fall of man described in Genesis 3. When Adam and Eve sinned against God, it brought death, disease, and the struggle for survival into the world. Mutations began to impact living things and cause disease. Mutations that cause cancer would never have been present before sin entered the world. In contrast, the evolutionary view teaches that mutations and the struggle for life are good because they brought about all of the life forms today. The Bible teaches us that God created the world as a perfect place and that sin has corrupted the world and that death and mutations are a part of that corruption. Our starting points always impact the way we understand the world, including mutations.

Natural Selection

Mutations produce variety—there is no doubt about that. As animals struggle to survive in the wild, some varieties will be able to survive better than others in certain environments. A mutation can lead to a variation of a trait that is beneficial in one environment and harmful in another. Imagine a dog that had a mutation in the hair-producing genes that caused the dog to have long hair. If that dog lived in a cold climate, it might be better able to survive the cold winters and would be more likely to reproduce more offspring with long hair. If it lived in a desert environment, the long hair mutation might cause it to overheat and die. After several generations, that mutation would disappear from the gene pool (or turn dormant).

This is an overly simple explanation of the process of natural selection. However, even if it works the way we imagine it, natural selection can only select from trait variations available within each organism. Natural selection cannot cause new traits to come about any more than climate changes can write new computer codes. Mutations can and do alter pre-existing biological code, however.

Like mutations, evolutionists use natural selection to attempt to explain how organisms could have adapted to different environments and changed from fish into amphibians over the course of millions of years. But this origins science question involves many assumptions about the past that can never be verified. The mutations and natural selection processes from the past can never be observed, measured, or repeated. These two processes are supposed to be able to cause one kind of animal to change into another, but scientists have not witnessed this. In other words, mutations change existing traits within a reproducing kind, but they don't change one kind into another—a distinction that textbooks always ignore. Let's look at some of the classic examples and see if they really demonstrate that new information can be added to the genome through these processes.

Finch Beaks

If you open just about any biology textbook to the section on natural selection and evolution, you are almost certain to find two examples that illustrate Natural Selection + Mutations + Time = Evolution. The first involves some very detailed research conducted over a long period of time on the Galapagos Islands. Peter and Rosemary Grant began their studies in the 1960s. They measured several aspects of the different finches living on the islands in the Pacific Ocean. One thing they noticed was that the shape of the finch beaks changed with different long-term climate changes.

In periods of drought, the island's seeds had thicker shells, so birds with thicker beaks were better able to crack the thick shells. Because they could eat, they survived and passed their genes on to their offspring. When the weather was wetter, the average finch beaks got more slender. They have clearly documented the process of changing variation in the beak sizes and shapes that matched prevailing weather patterns. If this was natural selection, was it also evolution in action? No, and here is why.

The size of the beaks goes up and down over the years, but it never permanently changes, and it certainly doesn't change into something other than a beak. In order for this to be "evolution in action," we should see some type of new physical feature or biological process. But all the Grants observed were skinny beaks changing into wide beaks and vice versa. Beaks remained beaks on birds that were previously birds. How is that evolution in action? Dr. John Morris sum it up this way:

> The two scholars, Drs. Peter and Rosemary Grant, observed how, under drought conditions, birds with larger beaks were better adapted than others, thus their percentage increased. But this trend reversed when the cyclical conditions reversed. Furthermore, in times of drought, the normally separate species were observed to cross-breed. They are related after all. Darwin was right! [in this part of the matter]. But

is this really evolution? Even after the changes there is still the same array of beak sizes and shapes. This is variation and adaptation, not evolution. Actually, de-evolution has occurred; the observation is that there are larger groupings of species into what may be more reminiscent of the originally created kind. Creation agrees with Darwin's observations and with the newer observations, but evolution doesn't, even though the Grants interpret this as rapid evolution. Wonderful study—great data, wrong interpretation.[140]

"Evolving" Bacteria

Another very popular example found in textbooks and news articles has to do with bacteria becoming resistant to antibiotics. Textbooks don't mention that what is happening in bacterial biology actually opposes what is needed for molecules-to-man evolution to happen.

Here is one common way that antibiotics interact with bacteria. When a bacterium absorbs an antibiotic, a bacterial enzyme breaks it down and turns it into a poison that kills the cell. Certain bacteria in a population may have a mutation that damages or diminishes the enzyme. When they absorb the antibiotic, they can't turn it into the poison so they survive—they are resistant to the antibiotic. So this is survival of the fittest, right? Well, yes—but the mutants are only more 'fit' when swimming in antibiotic. Normally, non-mutants grow much faster than the mutants because the enzyme in question actually performs a life-enhancing task when not used to convert antibiotics to poison. The bacteria that had a mutation survived in that environment. That is the formula for evolution, right?

Well, not exactly. In order for evolution to happen, there has to be an increase in information—new information has to be added to the genome. That is not what happens with these bacteria. The mutations have caused a *loss* of information—the ability to make a proper enzyme. Losing information can't lead to a gain in information. Antibiotic resistance is a great example of natural selection—observational science—but it is not an example of evolution over millions of years—historical science—because it does not generate so much as a single new gene, let alone a new organism.

A Biblical Alternative

Biology books often show a "tree of life" when describing the history of life on Earth. Their evolutionary authors believe that a single organism evolved into different kinds of organisms, branching out into different forms through mutations and the process of natural selection (despite the hurdles described above). One branch of the tree might show a palm and another an orangutan. But no one has seen this tree in actual life—it is a drawing to explain an idea that they believe. It is an idea that follows a certain philosophy—the philosophy of naturalism—and into which they force the evidence.

If we begin our thinking from the Word of God, as we should if we are to honor Christ, we have a very different way of interpreting the evidence. God describes how He created living things in the first chapter of the Bible—Genesis 1. He tells us, as an eyewitness to His own work, that He created plants and animals according to their kinds to reproduce after their kinds. Genesis 1:11 makes this clear: "Let the earth bring forth grass, the herb that yields seed, and the fruit tree that yields fruit according to its kind, whose seed is in itself, on the earth." God supernaturally and specially created the different kinds of plants with seeds to produce more of the same kind. A coconut will never sprout a plum tree. The passages describing animals teach the same thing (Genesis 1:20–25; 6:19–20).

So rather than a single tree of life, we could draw an orchard of trees each representing a distinct kind of plant or animal.[141] All of the branches on the tree represent the variation within those kinds that have resulted from different expressions of the initial genetic variation God programmed in the original organisms as well as later mutations and other forms of genetic mixing. This orchard model is also an idea developed from a certain philosophy—Biblical creation.

Both of these views offer explanations for the evidence that we have in the present, but only one can be correct. Each attempts to apply observational science to understand the history of life on earth. One problem with the evolutionary worldview is that it must rely on unprovable assumptions. In contrast, biblical creation begins from the eyewitness testimony of the Creator God as described in His trustworthy Word—the Bible. You can trust that God has created life on this Earth. He did it for a reason. And that means that He created you for a reason. You are not simply the result of random accidents and the laws of nature—God created you and offers you the opportunity to know Him through His Son, Jesus Christ (Colossians 2:1–10).

Though textbooks portray evolution as a natural process whereby naturally selected mutations build new and more complicated creatures over vast eons from old and simple ones, we have seen this formula fail. Nature can only select from the options organisms already possess, and mutations do not generate the options required to turn bacteria into finches, for example. The alternative origins explanation—biblical creation—fits the evidence just fine by explaining the original biological programming as having been created, and the constantly corrupting mutations as God's consequence for man's original sin.

Chapter 7:

Did Hippos Evolve into Whales?

Jonathan Sarfati, Ph.D. & Daniel A. Biddle, Ph.D.

Why is this Chapter Important?

Biology textbooks use illustrations of "ancient" land-dwelling mammals turning into modern whales over millions of years to illustrate their version of history—evolution. For example, Miller & Levine's high school biology textbook prominently displays six creatures leading up to modern whales.[142] This Chapter will review how these "pre-whale" animals don't line up in any such fashion. We will show instead that these fossils represent extinct marine or land animals that never evolved into whales. Further, we will review some impossibilities with the idea in secular circles that some wolf-sized animals evolved into 360,000-pound sea-dwelling whales. Even evolutionists' own models show that these changes cannot be made given their own timescale. In the end, we wish our readers to gain confidence in the fact that so-called "whale evolution" falls far short of what its proponents say about it. In fact, we hope you will see not only how evolution fails whales, but how well the fossils fit into biblical history.

Overview

Whales are one of God's most magnificent creations. They are even mentioned specifically in the King James Bible translation: "And God created great whales, and every living creature that moveth, which the waters brought forth abundantly, after their kind..." (Genesis 1:21).[143] To begin our discussion on the evolution of whales, let's begin with a quick description of what makes whales so unique.

Let's start first with the obvious—whales are massive. They are the largest animals on Earth, with the 100-foot long female blue whale at the top of the list. This animal weighs in at 360,000 pounds (the equivalent of 2,000 people), has a tongue the size and weight of an African elephant, and a heart that is the size of a small car that pumps 2,640 gallons of blood.[144]

Baleen whales have specially designed comb-like bristles in their mouths called "baleen" that enable them to eat tiny krill as they move through the ocean at speeds up to 30 miles per hour (requiring over 1,000 horsepower to do so!). Much of this power is generated by a tail that is 25 feet wide. Blue whales can dive over 1,500 feet and communicate with each other up to 1,000 miles away. Baleen whales feed by the enormously energetic process of 'lunge feeding,' and have a unique sensory organ to coordinate this so their jaws don't shatter. This organ senses the "dynamic rotation of the jaws during mouth opening and closure [and] provides the necessary input to the brain for coordinating the initiation, modulation and end stages of engulfment."[145] To say the least, these are amazing creatures.

Evolutionists insist that these wonderful marine creatures, outfitted as they are with an array of specifications precisely targeted for successful life in water, evolved from ancestors that once had none of those specifications. These people write state-sponsored textbooks, yet have plenty of explaining to do. How, step-by-step, and without using words like "evolution," "selection," or "emerged," could whales have evolved in the manner they describe?

Evolution faces a whale of a challenge, not just from a theoretical basis but from the standpoint of observational science. What creature kinds have served as the best candidates for evolutionary whale ancestry? The founder of the theory of evolution himself, Charles Darwin, had an idea. In the first edition (1865) of his well-known book, *The Origin of Species*, Darwin wrote:

> In North America the black bear was seen... swimming for hours with widely open mouth, thus catching, like a whale, insects in the water. Even in so extreme a case as this, if the supply of insects were constant, and if better adapted competitors did not already exist in the country, I can see no difficulty in a race of bears being rendered, by natural selection, more and more aquatic in their structure and habits, with larger and larger mouths, till a creature was produced as monstrous as a whale.[146]

While this section was removed from later editions of the book, in 1903 he stated that he still maintained his position of bears evolving into whales: "I still maintain that there is no special difficulty in a bear's mouth being enlarged to any degree useful to its changing habits."[147] Clearly, Darwin believed that any creature has an unlimited potential to change its form. He was wrong about this, and other places in this book tell why.

Fast-forward to the 1970s. Bears are now *out* of the evolutionary "whale line" and textbooks report other animal candidates as whale ancestors such as *Mesonychids,* known from fossils.[148] Then, in the 1980s, *Pakicetus* took first position.[149] Twenty years later, a large group of evolutionists selected the *hippopotamus,* while another group placed pigs into the "evolving" evolutionary ancestry of whales.[150]

What's next? Fortunately, from a biblical creation standpoint, God made whales on the Day 5 of Creation, each creature after their own *kind*. And this view hasn't changed since these words of Scripture were penned about *3,500 years ago*!

If whale evolution is true, then we would expect many other transitional "in-between" whale-like animals, either living or fossil, each stepping up along the evolutionary tree. Just take a look at the differences between some of these "starter" animals, which were land mammals, and the whales into which they supposedly evolved. As Dr. Carl Werner points out:

> Consider how miraculous it would be for a wolf or a bear or any such creature to evolve into the 13 families and 79 species of whales, from the finless porpoise measuring about four feet long, to the blue whale measuring 100 feet. The latter weighs 360,000 pounds (the equivalent of 2,000 people); its tongue is the size and weight of an African elephant; its heart is the size of a small car; its heart pumps 2,640 gallons of blood; and a human could swim through its massive aorta.[151]

A prominent evolutionary biologist now known for expressing doubt about some Darwinist claims, Dr. Richard Sternberg, studied whale evolution in depth. He concluded that there is simply not enough time within evolutionary time stamps to make *even a few of the changes* necessary to reorganize a land creature into a whale.[152] Some of these changes had to include:

- Counter-current heat exchanger for intra-abdominal testes (to keep them cool)
- Ball vertebra (to enable the tail to move up and down instead of side to side)
- Tail flukes and musculature
- Blubber for temperature insulation
- Ability to drink sea water (reorganization of kidney tissues)
- Nurse young underwater (modified mammae)
- Forelimbs transformed into flippers
- Reduction of hindlimbs
- Reduction/loss of pelvis and sacral vertebrae
- Reorganization of the musculature for the reproductive organs
- Hydrodynamic properties of the skin
- Special lung surfactants
- Novel muscle systems for the blowhole
- Modification of the teeth
- Modification of the eye for underwater vision
- Emergence and expansion of the mandibular fat pad with complex lipid distribution
- Reorganization of skull bones and musculature
- Modification of the ear bones
- Decoupling of esophagus and trachea
- Synthesis and metabolism of isovaleric acid (toxic to terrestrial mammals)

In a debate regarding the origins of life, Dr. Sternberg stated, "How could this process alone have produced fully aquatic cetaceans (whales) with their multiple, anatomical novelties, requiring many hundreds, even thousands of adaptive changes in less than 2 million years—even less than 9 million years?... I'm saying it doesn't add up."[153] We would need thousands of in-between examples of fossils demonstrating *each* of these requirements developing through time.

Making this evolutionary process even more difficult to believe, the jawbone of an ancient whale found in Antarctica in October 2011 was "dated" to 49 million years, which would imply that the first fully-developed whales now date to about the same time as one of the supposed whale "ancestors," named *Ambulocetus*.[154]

It is clear that what we have on Earth is a *created* "kind" of whales that have existed since Day 5 of Creation, and not some evolutionary line of land-mammals leading to the largest creature on Earth—a 360,000 pound blue whale that is able to swim up to 30 miles per hour, has a tongue that weighs as much as an elephant, a heart the size of a car, eats 4–8 tons of krill each day, and dives to depths of over 1,500 feet while holding its breath. By now, it should become clear that it takes more faith to believe in evolution than it does in whale Creation.

With this background in mind, we will next review and reject each of the animals that are supposedly linked together in the successive train of whale evolution.

Animals (that Don't Belong) in the Progression of Whale Evolution

Several high school and college biology textbooks display the supposed "whale evolution" model by putting several pictures of extinct and living animals side-by-side and bonding them together in a hypothetical evolutionary explanation that one animal led to the next, on up the evolutionary tree. For example, the first two in Miller & Levine's line-up (Ancient artiodactyls and *Pakicetus*) are land-dwelling mammals (similar to wolves), the next two (*Ambulocetus* and *Rodhocetus*) allegedly started developing fins and tails/flippers, the next two (*Basilosaurus* and *Dorudon*) are early whales, followed by the two suborders of modern whales: Mysticeti (baleen whales) and Odontoceti (toothed whales).[155] Lined up this way, they seem to tell a neat evolutionary story. But as we will show, this arrangement follows more from an underlying philosophical commitment to evolution than to scientific data.

From a biblical creationist standpoint, these eight mammals are not related and have not evolved. Rather, the first two are simply extinct wolf-like creatures most likely buried and later fossilized by Noah's Flood, the next four are extinct whale-like creatures (which also likely died in the Flood), and the last two are obviously whales that still exist today.

Asserting that these eight animals are somehow all tied to the same evolutionary tree is similar to digging up a golf ball, baseball, and soccer ball in your backyard and saying, "See! This must be proof of ball evolution!" Just because animals shared some similar features or habitats does not mean that they are related, or that one led to the other! After all, nobody has ever observed a progression of one kind evolving into another. As discussed in Chapter 6, animals can and do *adapt* by making certain adjustments, such as "Darwin's Finches," but they do not change from one kind of animal to another. Indeed, Darwin's Finches are still finches—they differ only by beak size and shape. The same is true with whales.

Each of these "evolving whale" creatures will be discussed below, along with some amazing recent admissions made by the evolutionists who originally touted them as "proof" of evolution.

Ancient artiodactyl

"Artiodactyl" is a collective term used to mean "even-toed" animals, referring to their two or four hoofs per foot. According to evolutionary fossil-age assignments, they date back some 54 million years. Animals in this category include goats, sheep, camels, pigs, cows, and deer. Other than just saying so, there is no evidence connecting this entire group of animals to whales. By suggesting that whales evolved from some "ancient artiodactyl," they implicitly admit that they do not have a real fossil connecting whales to other mammals, instead reaching for an imaginary, not-yet-found "ancestor."

Pakicetus

Pakicetus means "whale from Pakistan," but it looked nothing like a whale. It was originally represented by a few elongated *wolf-like skull fragments* that were first discovered by paleontologist Philip Gingerich in the early 1980s.[156] Based on these skull fragments, Gingerich asserted that the *Pakicetus* was a "perfect intermediate" between land animals and whales.[157] Drawings of the *Pakicetus* swimming in the ocean as a sea creature soon adorned standardized textbooks.[158] At the time, it was easy to pretend that *Pakicetus* had a whale-like body, since we had no body fossils.

About ten years later, more *Pakicetus* fossils were discovered, including additional body fossils associated with skull material. "All the postcranial bones indicate that pakicetids were land mammals... Many of the fossils' features... indicate that the animals were runners, moving with only their digits touching the ground," according to the prestigious journal *Nature*.[159] These led to the conclusion that the *Pakicetus* was "no more amphibious than a tapir"[160] Tapirs are modern browsing mammals living in South America, similar to pigs but with longer snouts. Once new fossils showed that it had well-organized, fast-running legs, was *Pakicetus* immediately removed from its iconic whale ancestry position in evolutionary textbook diagrams? Surprisingly, texts often still include *Pakicetus*. This is just bad science. Tapirs are alive today, and no one has seen these animals evolving at all, much less to anything close to a sea-dwelling whale. A recent article in *National Geographic* reports that Gingerich now believes that whales are related to antelopes based on a "single piece of fossil" found in 2000.[161]

Just viewing the illustration of the *Pakicetus* in common biology textbooks shows these animals to have simply been extinct, wolf-like mammals.

Ambulocetus

Ambulocetus is based on a set of fossil fragments that was discovered in Pakistan in 1993. To date there have been *only two Ambulocetus* fossils found.[162] One high school biology textbook includes this creature in whale evolution by stating: "The limb structure of *Ambulocetus* 'walking whale' suggests that these animals could both swim in shallow water and walk on land."[163]

Alligators and crocodiles are reptiles that look similar to the mammal *Ambulocetus*, and they can swim and walk on land. Why have they not also been lined up in the evolutionary train leading to whales?

In his book, *Evolution: A Theory in Crisis*, evolutionary biochemist, Dr. Michael Denton, points out that *Ambulocetus'* backbone ends in the pelvic bone (from which powerful leg bones extend), which is typical for land mammals. In whales, on the other hand, the backbone continues right down to the tail and there is no pelvic bone at all. *Basilosaurus*, thought to have lived up to 10 million years after *Ambulocetus*, possesses a typical no-pelvis whale anatomy. There is no intermediate form between *Ambulocetus*, a typical terrestrial animal, and *Basilosaurus*, a typical whale. Note also that *Basilosaurus* is about 10 times longer than *Ambulocetus*, although evolutionary textbooks often draw them side-by-side to make the 'transitional series' look better. *Basilosaurus* and sperm whales have small bones independent of the backbone in their lower bodies. Some evolutionists claim that these are shrunken leg bones. However, the bones in question more likely had functional uses in reproduction in *Basilosaurus*, whereas in sperm whales they support the reproductive organs.[164] Why would they have evolved into legs if they were already useful in their present state?

Dr. Carl Werner points out that the evolution "evidence" involving *Ambulocetus* consists of nothing more than *just by saying so*:

> According to Dr. Annalisa Berta, an expert in aquatic mammal evolution, "*Ambulocetus is a whale by virtue of its inclusion in that lineage*." In other words, *Ambulocetus* was defined as a "walking whale" not because it had a whale's tail or a whale's flippers or a blowhole, but because [some] evolution scientists believed it was on the line to becoming a whale, it became a "whale." And since it was a land animal with four legs, it was then called a "walking whale." Scientists who oppose evolution are quick to point out that this reasoning is circular and therefore specious.[165] (emphasis added)

Dr. Werner also pointed out that because *Ambulocetus* has eyes on the top of its head (like a crocodile) it should be clearly classified as a mammal with legs, having nothing to do with whales.

Rodhocetus

Rodhocetus was also found in Pakistan in 1992, and is now represented by three fossils.[166] The most well-known *Rodhocetus* is made up of two partial skeletons that make up an "early whale" that had short limbs, long hands, and feet.[167] The Levine & Miller biology textbook states that its hind limbs were "short and probably not able to bear much weight. Paleontologists think that these animals spent most of their time in the water."[168]

Many of the textbook illustrations of the *Rodocetus* show it with legs and a dolphin or a common whale tail. For example, the *Proceedings of the National Academy of Sciences* showed *Rodhocetus* with a fluked tail similar to a typical whale.[169] Several other textbooks followed the practice, making for a convincing presentation that this animal (all three of them) was some type of transition step along the way to today's whales.

Dr. Phil Gingerich, the paleontologist most responsible for the reconstruction and presentation of *Rodhocetus, added* a prominent tail and "fluke" (the wide fin at the end of the tail) to *Rodhocetus* when it was displayed at the Natural History Museum at the University of Michigan. When interviewed about why he added a whale fluke on *Rodhocetus*, Dr. Gingerich answered, "Well, I told you we don't have the tail in *Rodhocetus*. So, we don't know for sure whether it had a ball vertebrae indicating a fluke or not. So, I speculated it might have had a fluke."[170]

During this same revealing interview, Dr. Gingerich also acknowledged that the flippers were drawn on the diagram without fossil representation! Today he no longer believes that this animal had flippers, stating, "Since then we have found the forelimbs, the hands, and the front arms of *Rodhocetus*, and we understand that it doesn't have the kind of arms that can spread out like flippers on a whale." Without flippers or tail, *Rodhocetus* should be removed from its evolutionary lineup. The way its features had been imaginatively added, like those of *Pakicetus* before more complete fossils were found, clearly show whale evolution to be a product of researchers' minds and not of scientific observation.

Basilosaurus

A total of over 100 *Basilosaurus* fossils have been found around the world including Egypt, Jordan, Pakistan, and in the United States (Mississippi and Alabama). One of the features that led evolutionists to believe that the *Basilosaurus* should be included in the "whale evolution line" are its hind "limbs."[171] Evolutionists frequently represent these limbs as "leftovers" from a supposed land-dwelling past. They supposedly lost their legs, evolved flippers, and became whales.

However, many leading evolutionists are now admitting that these limbs, like the small "leftover" limbs in "modern" whales, "could only be some kind of sexual or reproductive clasper."[172] These "claspers" are necessary to join multi-ton animals tightly together while mating in water and swimming, a design found in numerous other sea creatures. Whale evolutionist Dr. Gingerich wrote:

> Hind limbs of *Basilosaurus* appear to have been too small relative to body size... to have assisted in swimming, and they could not possibly have supported the body on land. However, maintenance of some function is likely... The pelvis of modern whales [not a limb-supporting "pelvis"] serves to anchor reproductive organs, even though functional hind limbs are lacking. Thus hind limbs of Basilosaurus are most plausibly interpreted as accessories facilitating reproduction.[173]

It is also interesting that apparently no transitional fossils between current whales and the *Basilosaurus* have been found, even though hundreds of each have been found. If evolution is true, one would think that over 35 million years of evolution would have produced some fossilized examples of transitions, but the fossil record "jumps" from

Basilosaurus, which was a fully aquatic animal, to modern whales, with nothing in between.[174] In actuality, God created whales and *Basilosaurus* separately.

Dorudon

There have been over 50 *Dorudon* fossils discovered around the world. These animals are simply extinct whales. They had nostril openings (blowholes) on top of their skulls, measured about 50 feet long, and lived in the water full-time. I described them in an online article that I wrote in 2008:

> The *Dorudon* was once classified as a juvenile *Basilosaurus*, since they are very similar, long, slender marine mammals, but *Dorudon* was 5 m long and *Basilosaurus* 18 m. They are now classified as separate subfamilies of Basolosauridae. They are most likely varieties of the same created kind, much as the false killer whale (*Pseudorca crassidens*) and a bottlenose dolphin (*Tursiops truncatus*) are the same biological species given that they can produce a fertile hybrid called a wholphin...the serpentine body structure, cheek teeth and nasal bones mean that it could not have been an ancestor to modern whales. Also, the allegedly vestigial hind limbs actually had an important function as reproductive claspers.[175]

Finally, Mysticetes include grey, blue, and humpback whales, and Odontocetes include toothed whales like dolphins and sperm whales. These modern whales are already whales, so have no place in whale evolution.

Summary

One of the certain facts that we can know from fossils is that *the animal died.* However, fossils do not come with tags showing the year they were created or buried in mud. When the evolutionist assumptions are removed, we no longer have a string of animals that led one to the other. Rather, we have various created kinds of animals that died by rapid muddy burials and then fossilized when the mud later dried.

What we can know for certain regarding the supposed story of whale evolution is that its theories have often changed—bears, mesonychids, *Pakicetus*, and now hippopotamuses have rotated through. The biblical viewpoint, however, remains *unchanged* since penned about 3,500 years ago: Whales were created as whales that can express variations within each of their kinds: some died off (many did not survive the Flood), and many are still alive today. Figure 19 shows how Biblical Creation has maintained a solid, unchanging perspective regarding the origin of whales, compared to the changing ideas of evolutionary theory.

Figure 19. Creation Theories about Whales

<table>
<tr><th colspan="8">Creation Theories about Whales</th></tr>
<tr><td>Time line</td><td>>4000 B.C.</td><td>3000 B.C.</td><td>2000 B.C.</td><td>1000 B.C.</td><td>0</td><td>1000 A.D.</td><td>Present Day</td></tr>
<tr><td rowspan="4">Evolutionary Perspective</td><td colspan="6" rowspan="4">Undetermined</td><td>Bears?</td></tr>
<tr><td>Pakicetus?</td></tr>
<tr><td>Antelopes?</td></tr>
<tr><td>Hippos?</td></tr>
<tr><td>Biblical Creation</td><td colspan="7">God Intentionally Created Whales by Design</td></tr>
</table>

Finally, considering the number of changes that are needed to turn a wolf, bear, hippopotamus, or pig into a 360,000 pound, 100-foot blue whale doesn't even pass the common sense test. It takes more faith to believe in that type of evolution than it does to believe in biblical creation. The multiple families of whales we have were simply created that way. Dr. Duane Gish describes such "incredible faith in the evolution" this way:

> Evolutionists are forced to believe that whatever the need may be, no matter how complex and unusual, random genetic errors were able to produce the structures required in a perfectly coordinated manner... It requires an enormous faith in miracles, where materialist philosophy actually forbids them, to believe that some hairy, four-legged mammal crawled into the water and gradually, over eons of time, gave rise to whales, dolphins, sea cows, seals, sea lions, walruses, and other marine mammals via thousands and thousands of random genetic errors. This blind hit and miss method supposedly generated the many highly specialized complex organs and structures without which these whales could not function, complex structures which in incipient stages would be totally useless and actually detrimental. Evolution theory is an incredible faith.[176]

Few of the members depicted in textbook illustrations of whale evolution belong there. Each shows evidence that it was a uniquely created creature, having no anatomical link to whales. Instead of showcasing evolution, the wonderful and integrated design features that make whale life possible should showcase their great Creator, the God of the Bible.

Chapter 8a:

Are Humans and Chimps Really 99% Similar? (Basic Level)

Daniel A. Biddle, Ph.D.

Why is this Chapter Important?

One of the great trophies that evolutionists often parade is the assertion that human and chimp DNA are 98–99% similar.[177] A quick Internet search will reveal this quip in hundreds of places, including school text books, blogs, videos, and journals. Because it sounds so compelling—like a proof of evolution just by saying so—we will take a look at the "chimp-human-99% similar" issue from an objective standpoint, being responsible to both the Bible and science.

To do so, this Chapter is broken into three sections. This first section covers only some basic observations and practical insights. Drs. Wile and Tomkins provide the next two sections which offer intermediate- and advanced-level discussions regarding the DNA similarities and differences between humans and chimps.

A Basic Overview regarding Human and Chimp Differences and Similarities

God made the chimp "kind" (which currently includes four species) as a *soul-less*, created animal on Day 6 of creation. Then, on the same Day, God made a single man in His own image, gave him an eternal *soul* (Genesis 2:7), and commanded him to "rule over the fish in the sea and the birds in the sky, over the livestock and all the wild animals," including chimps (Genesis 1:26).

If the creation narrative from the Bible is true, we would expect to see *exactly* what we see in today's ape-kinds. First, several varieties or species of chimps have no regard for eternity. For example, they do not bury their dead or conduct funeral rituals. Second, apes use very limited verbal communication—they do not write sentences. Third, and most importantly, they do not have *spiritual or religious practices* like humans do. In other words, they show no need or capacity for knowing their spiritual creator through worship or prayer. This seems to fit very well with the biblical creation account (i.e., man is a created, spiritual being with a soul).

Now, let's take a look at the physical side—the DNA issue. For starters, do you think that God, in his desire to create diverse life on Earth, would start with the same building materials like DNA and protein sequences for making various animal kinds, or would He start from scratch each time? DNA research has revealed that He used similar building blocks for the various life He created on Earth. In fact, we see this in nature, too—with many plants sharing Fibonacci spirals (clear numerical patterns) and sequences as basic building blocks and patterns that God used in His creation.

Let's consider for a minute just how efficient God's design is regarding the supposed human-chimp DNA similarities. Somehow, God was able to create *very different beings* out of similar DNA because they are built by God's own building blocks! So, even if they do share similarities, this is no different than a master automotive engineer being able to make a Volkswagen bug or a Porsche Carrera out of the same 2-ton block of raw steel. The same raw materials can be used by a master engineer to produce two very different types of automobiles. Next let's take a look at just how different chimps and humans are, even though they share some similar DNA.

When compared to chimps, humans are about 38% taller, 80% heavier, live 50% longer, and have brains that are about 400% larger (1330 ccs compared to 330 ccs).[178] Isn't it amazing how such an alleged 1–2% difference in DNA can result in such drastic differences? Some additional differences are highlighted below:

- Chimps show aggression by showing their teeth; people smile to show warmth.
- Humans communicate using an elaborate and sophisticated verbal and physical communication system; chimps lack even the basic muscle and nervous design construction in their vocal chords, tongues, lips, and brains to do so.
- When it comes to reproduction and sex, only humans experience jealousy or competition; chimps typically mate with multiple short-term partners.
- Humans walk upright; chimps are knuckle-walkers.
- Humans design and use highly complex tools and multi-component systems; chimps only use basic tools, and *not even as cleverly as crows do at that!*
- Humans adapt their surroundings to themselves; chimps adapt themselves to their surroundings.
- Humans have directed and systematic ways for educating the next generation; education is mostly indirect and not premeditated with chimps.

- Humans have uniquely human feet; Chimps have hands for feet.
- Humans make human babies; chimps make only chimp babies.

Thus, even if human and chimpanzee DNA sequences are as similar as textbooks and other evolution-inspired outlets insist—and as you will learn in the next section, they are not—a wide range of actual differences clearly showcase uniquely designed kinds. Many of these differences are obvious, as we will see in more detail.

At the time of this writing, emerging research was being released by Dr. David A. DeWitt ("What about the Similarity Between Human and Chimp DNA?" AnswersinGenesis.com: http://www.answersingenesis.org/articles/nab3/human-and-chimp-dna [January 14, 2014]) that revealed new stunning insights regarding the differences between human and chimp DNA:

> There are 40–45 million bases present in humans that are missing from chimps and about the same number present in chimps that are absent from man. These extra DNA nucleotides are called "insertions" or "deletions" because they are thought to have been added to or lost from the original sequence. This puts the total number of DNA differences at about 125 million. However, since the insertions can be more than one nucleotide long, there are about 40 million total separate mutation events that would separate the two species in the evolutionary view. To put this number into perspective, a typical 8½ x 11-inch page of text might have 4,000 letters and spaces. It would take 10,000 such pages full of text to equal 40 million letters! So the difference between humans and chimpanzees includes about 35 million DNA bases

> that are different, about 45 million in the human that are absent from the chimp, and about 45 million in the chimp that are absent from the human.

Such research continues to reveal that we are much, much different than chimps! In fact, these "10,000 pages" of different DNA programming is enough to fill the pages of 20, full-sized novels! There is no doubt that God has a specific set of DNA programming for humans, and another for chimps.

Chapter 8b:

DNA Evidence: Are Humans and Chimps Really 99% Similar? (Intermediate Level)

Jay L. Wile, Ph.D.

Overview

In this chapter, you will learn that the genetic similarity between chimpanzees and humans isn't anywhere close to what most evolutionists claim. Rather than being 99% similar when it comes to their genomes, humans and chimpanzees are roughly 70% similar. This is important, because evolution claims that the common ancestor between humans and chimpanzees existed roughly six million years ago. As a result, all of the genetic difference between the two must be explained by a mere six million years of evolution. Both genomes are so large, however, that it is extremely difficult to imagine how such a big difference could be produced on such a short evolutionary timescale. Honest assessment of the available evidence clearly shows that evolutionary ideas fall short, and that humans and chimps are distinctly different creations design by God.

Comparing Human and Chimp DNA

Evolutionists tell us that apes and humans evolved from a common ancestor that is supposed to have existed about six million years ago. That common ancestor supposedly gave rise to both the modern apes (like gorillas and chimpanzees) as well as people. As a result, humans and apes are supposed to be very closely related. Of all the living apes, the chimpanzee is supposed to be our closest living relative.

According to many evolutionists, humans and chimps share 99% of their DNA. Indeed, Dr. Jonathan Silvertown and several other scientists teamed up to write a book entitled *99% Ape: How Evolution Adds Up*.[179] In that book they say, "We share about 99% of our DNA with chimps, and this common ancestry has the deepest implications for how we see ourselves." This "fact" is so widely taught that the TV program NOVA informs us, "Today, many a schoolchild can cite the figure perhaps most often called forth in support of [a common ancestor between apes and humans]—namely, that we share almost 99% of our DNA with our closest living relative, the chimpanzee."[180] The problem is that the science of genetics tells us something *quite different*.

In order for you to understand how chimpanzee and human DNA compare, you first need to know a few things about genetics. Let's start with the structure of DNA. While it's an incredibly complicated molecule, its important features are surprisingly simple. It has a chemical backbone that is wound in a double-helix structure, as shown in Figure 20.

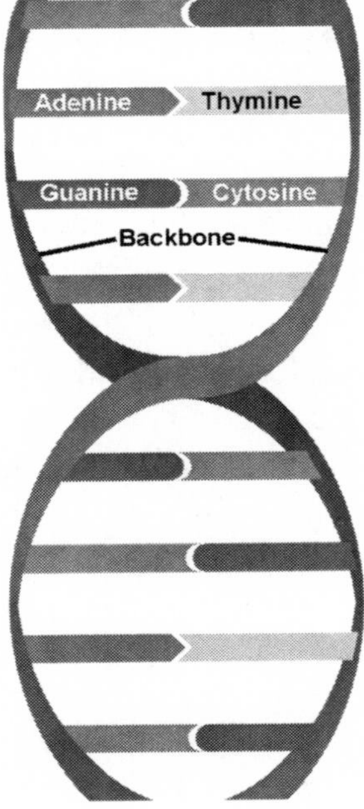

Figure 20. DNA Design

Even though this chemical backbone is important for the molecule, it is not important for the purposes of our discussion. In the end, the only thing you need to worry about is what holds this double helix together.

As mentioned in Chapter 6 on natural selection, there are four chemical units that lock together and hold the backbone in this double-helix shape. They are called "nucleotide bases," and their names are "adenine," "thymine," "guanine," and "cytosine." As shown in the illustration, they link together so that adenine is always linked to thymine and guanine is always linked to cytosine. When they link together like that, they are called a "base pair." The sequence of base pairs forms a language code, just like the sequence of letters on a page. It stores all the information a creature needs to live. So when we compare the DNA of two different creatures, we are comparing the sequence of base pairs found in their DNA.

Where is this DNA found? Every living thing is made up of basic units called "cells," and the DNA is stored in the cell's control center, which is called the "nucleus." Some living things, like amoebae, have only one cell. However, most of the creatures with which we are familiar are made of billions of cells. The human body is made of trillions of cells. Each one of those cells has the same DNA in its nucleus, and we call that collection of DNA the creature's "genome." So when you hear a phrase like "the human genome," it is referring to all DNA that is contained in the nucleus of a human cell.

With that terminology under your belt, you are more ready to understand how we can compare human and chimp DNA. First, we have to figure out the sequence of base pairs in the human genome. Second, we have to figure out the sequence of base pairs in the chimp genome. Then, we compare one sequence to the other. The more base pair sequences that match, the more similar the genomes are.

This is where we come to our first problem in comparing the two genomes: we don't know exactly what the sequence of base pairs is in either one of them! When a genome is sequenced, scientists don't start at the beginning and determine each base pair until they get to the end. We can't analyze DNA that way, because our technology isn't sophisticated enough yet. Instead, we have to take the DNA and chop it up into little chunks that are generally less than 1,000 base pairs long. When that happens, the *order* of these chunks is lost. As a result, a sequenced genome just consists of a lot of chunks. The scientists then try to piece those chunks together using computer software after they have been decoded. This is called "genome assembly," and it is a terribly difficult task.

It turns out that genome assembly is so difficult that it is hard to determine exactly when you are done. If you assemble a genome one way, you'll get one set of base pairs, and if you do it a slightly different way, you will get a slightly different set of base pairs. Because of this, we don't even know for sure *how many* base pairs are in the human genome. At this point in time, the best scientists can say is that it is made up of somewhere between 3.1 and 3.3 billion base pairs.[181] It probably contains some number in between. We just don't know for sure. In the end, then, we only know the human genome to a precision of 94%.

We can say a similar thing about the chimpanzee genome. To the best of our knowledge, the chimp genome contains somewhere between 3.0 and 3.3 billion base pairs. As a result, we only know the chimp genome to a precision of 90%. Now that should tell you something right away. If we only know the human genome to an accuracy of 94%, and we only know the chimp genome to an accuracy of 90%, there is simply no way we can say that they are 99% similar! We would have to know both of them with nearly 100% accuracy before we could make such a statement! So in the end, it is simply *impossible* for current scientists to claim that the two genomes are 99% similar.

So what *can* scientists safely say about the two genomes? Well, they can compare the parts of the genomes that we know very well and determine how similar those parts are. A genome can be split into two basic parts: protein-coding DNA and non-protein-coding DNA. The protein-coding DNA is generally referred to as "genes," and these parts of the DNA are like little recipes. They give the cell all the information it needs to make chemicals that we call "proteins."

It turns out that only a small percentage of a cell's genome is protein-coding. The human genome, for example, devotes less than 2% of its base pairs to protein-coding. The other 98% is non-protein-coding DNA. Scientists have been studying the protein-coding part of the genome (the genes) the longest, so we understand it a lot better than we understand the non-protein-coding DNA. Since we know the protein-coding DNA the best, let's start there. How similar are the protein-coding segments in the human and chimpanzee genomes? Are they 99% similar?

After both the human and chimpanzee genomes were sequenced, scientists compared the genes in the human genome to the genes in the chimpanzee genome. Many were very similar, and many were exactly the same. However, several genes were found in the chimpanzee genome that could not be found anywhere in the human genome. In the same way, several genes were found in the human genome that could not be found anywhere in the chimp genome. The conclusion of the study was, "humans and chimpanzees differ by at least 6% (1,418 of 22,000 genes) in their complement of genes."[182] So even when you concentrate on *just the genes*, humans and chimpanzees are at most only 94% similar.

Of course, the genes make up less than 2% of the genome, so that really doesn't tell us much about how similar humans and chimpanzees are on a genetic level. After all, we know the cell uses the non-coding DNA, so it must be important. We don't understand it very well, but since the cell uses it, we should include it in the analysis. What happens then? At that point, the similarity drops significantly!

In 2008, geneticist Dr. Richard Buggs from Queen Mary University of London wrote an analysis of the similarities between the entire human genome (that we know to an accuracy of 94%) and the entire chimpanzee genome (that we know to an accuracy of 90%). He said that only 2.4 billion of the chimpanzee base pairs could be reasonably lined up against the 3.1 billion base pairs in the human genome. Even in that lineup, however, there were still some mismatches. In the end, the best he could do was come up with a 72% similarity between the human and chimpanzee genomes. But even that number is too high a number, because some sequences appeared once in one genome and more than once in the other genome. In the end, he said, "Therefore the total similarity of the genomes could be below 70%."[183]

In February of 2013, Dr. Jeffery Tomkins, a former director of the Clemson University Genomics Institute performed an extremely detailed comparison of the human and chimpanzee genomes. To understand his analysis completely, you need to know that when cells reproduce, they arrange their DNA into small packets called "chromosomes." These chromosomes come in pairs, and while humans have 23 pairs of chromosomes, chimpanzees have 24 pairs.

Now since evolutionists assume that humans and chimps share a common ancestor, they think that the creature which eventually evolved into both chimps and humans had 24 pairs of chromosomes. During the course of human evolution, however, two of those chromosome pairs merged to become just one chromosome pair. As a result, evolutionists think they can point to 22 human chromosome pairs that are directly related to 22 chimpanzee chromosome pairs. In addition, they think that one chromosome pair in humans is directly related to two chromosome pairs in chimpanzees.

In order to compare the human and chimpanzee genomes, Dr. Tomkins first digitally chopped each already-published chimpanzee chromosome into shorter segments. He then went to the human chromosome that evolutionists say is directly related to the chimpanzee chromosome. He searched that human chromosome for the closest match to each of his short chimpanzee chromosome segments. Last, he determined what percentage of the base pairs matched up exactly within each closest matching segment.

In other words, what Dr. Tomkins did was a *chromosome-by-chromosome* comparison between the two genomes. What he found was that the highest similarity between two chromosomes was 78%, and the lowest similarity was 43%. In the end, the overall similarity between the genomes was a mere 70%.[184] This agrees with the analysis done by Dr. Buggs.

So in the end, we have two comparisons of the human and chimpanzee genomes indicating that on the genetic level, they are only 70% similar. Now that sounds like a lot, but remember, each genome has more than 3 billion base pairs! This means that in the human genome, there are more than a billion base pairs that are different from what is found in the chimpanzee genome.

From an evolutionary point of view, it is extremely hard to understand how such a huge number of differences could arise. After all, mutations are supposed to be the driving force of evolution. So, more than a billion base pairs would have to change by mutation over the course of human and chimpanzee evolution. But evolutionists say that this process started "only" six million years ago. If over a billion base pairs have to mutate in six million years, that's an average of *167 mutations every year*! It's hard to understand how two species could survive such a high mutation rate, even if they shared it the entire way.

But wait a minute. Where did this 99% figure come from, anyway? If humans and chimpanzees really are only 70% similar on a genetic level, how in the world could anyone ever think that they are 99% similar? The answer is simple: *The 99% figure is more than 30 years out of date*! Back in 1975, Mary-Claire King and A. C. Wilson compared some proteins found in humans to the same proteins found in chimpanzees. They determined that, for the proteins they chose, the similarity was 99%. Well, scientists reasoned, the makeup of proteins is determined by DNA. So if the proteins are 99% similar, the DNA is 99% similar as well.[185]

Do you see the problem with that reasoning? Proteins are determined by genes, and the genes make up less than 2% of the genome. So King and Wilson were looking at chemicals produced by only a small fraction of the DNA. In addition, they only looked at proteins that appeared in *both* humans *and* chimps. As discussed earlier, there are lots of genes in chimps that aren't found in humans, and *vice versa*.

So in the end, King and Wilson's comparison applied to a ridiculously small amount of the genome. No wonder it wasn't even close to correct! The human genome was sequenced in the year 2000, and since then, several corrections have been made to that sequence. The chimpanzee genome was sequenced in 2005, and several corrections have been made to that sequence as well. In the end, it is simply not honest for evolutionists to continue to use a similarity percentage that was determined 30 years before both genomes were sequenced!

Why do evolutionists do this? Why do they continue to use the results of an outdated and incorrect study when discussing the similarity between the human and chimpanzee genomes? I am sure some do it out of ignorance, but there are also some who do it specifically because they know that the more recent studies show how vastly different humans and chimpanzees are on the genetic level. That's something evolutionists either are not prepared to admit or don't want you to know!

Chapter 8c:

DNA Evidence: Are Humans and Chimps Really 99% Similar? (Advanced Level)

Jeffrey Tomkins, Ph.D.

Introduction

Your high-school or college biology textbook will typically tell you that you are descended from sort of ape ancestor related to the great apes. This group of animals consists of gibbons, orangutans, gorillas, and chimpanzees. Of these apes, your textbook may also tell you that you are most closely related to a chimpanzee and that comparisons of human DNA to chimps proves it. So what is one result of this idea in recent history?

The real world consequences of this ideology involve humans not being considered anything more than just evolved animals by people that believe they are superior or "more evolved" that have the reins of power. This has been a primary foundation for the mistreatment and murder of humans worldwide by wicked genocidal political leaders and governments over the past 150 or so years of human history. One highly read study showed that the leading cause of death in the 20th century was "Democide"—or "murder by government," which has claimed over 260 million lives.[186] All of the totalitarian murderous tyrannies the world over, despite their different political variations, maintained the same Darwinian evolutionary philosophy that humans are nothing more than animals to be herded and culled in wars, death-camps, abortions, mass starvations, and outright slaughter.

Is the evil ideology that some humans are move evolved while others are nothing but just common animals really supported by the new science of DNA sequencing and genomics, or is it proving to be a completely fake paradigm? If this question is important to you—and it should be as a member of the human family—you will read this chapter very carefully. Once you fully understand the new DNA evidence debunking the alleged human evolution paradigm, you should better appreciate that you are a unique creation who the Creator made in His own image—special and unique among all other forms of creation.

Even when a child sees a chimpanzee, they can tell that it is radically different from a human and immediately realize that it is just a type of animal and not another person. And of course, scientists also realize that chimpanzees are radically different than humans in many different ways besides their outward appearance. Humans and chimpanzees have different bone structures and different types of brains, and there are even major physiological differences. Humans also have the ability to express their thoughts abstractly in speech, writing, and music, as well as develop other complicated systems of expression and communication. This is why humans stand above all other types of creatures and, as stated in the Bible, were created in the image of God.

Despite these clear differences between humans and apes, we have been repeatedly told by an array of mainstream outlets like high school and college biology textbooks that human and chimpanzee DNA is 98 to 99% similar. Are we really just a few genetic changes from being an ape? And what is the field of modern genetics research actually revealing? The answers may surprise you.

The fact of the matter is that when experts talk about DNA similarity they can be referring to a variety of different things. Sometimes scientists talk about humans and chimpanzees having the same genes while at other times they talk about their DNA sequences being 98 to 99% similar. First, let's talk about whether the actual DNA sequence of the chromosomes between humans and chimpanzees is really 98% similar. And after that, we will talk about the concept of genes and gene similarity, and what that really means to the whole issue of human and chimp DNA similarity.

Reality of DNA and Genome Similarity

As discussed in Dr. Wile's section, DNA occurs as chromosomes in humans, plants, and animals. They contain millions of these DNA bases in a specific order which forms a complex set of informational instructions called the "genetic code." In humans, there are two sets of chromosomes, one from the mother and one from the father. Each distinct set of chromosomes has 3 billion bases of information in it. In total, we all have 6 billion bases of DNA sequence in our chromosomes inside nearly every cell of our bodies. But even this is being conservative, because DNA is a double-stranded molecule and has encoded information on both strands running in different directions. In reality, each cell in your body actually has 12 billion bases of very complex DNA code in it!

When scientists talk about a creature's genome, they are actually only referring to one set of chromosomes, which helps simplify things a bit. Thus, in humans, the reference genome is the sum total of one set of 23 chromosomes. The

DNA sequence of the human genome was initially published in 2001, but it was only labeled an "initial draft" (preliminary version) as there were parts of the genome that were still not completely decoded. In 2004, scientists published another more complete version, but even then there were still small parts that remained incomplete. Not surprisingly, researchers are still updating the human genome on a regular basis as the DNA sequencing technologies improve and more data is acquired. Without a doubt, the human genome is probably one of the most complete and accurate of all known genome sequences–mostly because considerably more research money has been spent on it compared to other creatures.

Scientists initially decided to choose chimpanzees as the closest creature to humans based on both similarity of general features and because they knew early on that their proteins and DNA fragments had similar biochemical properties.[187] These ideas were first solidified just prior to the modern era of DNA sequencing. However, it wasn't always a clear-cut issue and there were different factions of researchers that wanted to choose gorillas or orangutans as being closest to humans. In fact, a recent research paper was still making the claim that orangutans were more similar to humans in structure and appearance than chimpanzees, and thus should be considered our closest ancestor. Nevertheless, the consensus opinion among evolutionary scientists is that chimpanzees are closest to humans on the hypothetical evolutionary tree.

In the early days of DNA sequencing in the 1970s and 1980s, scientists could only sequence very short segments of DNA because the technology was just beginning. Therefore, they focused on segments of DNA that they knew would be highly similar between animals, such as globin proteins from blood and mitochondrial DNA (DNA which is inherited from the mother). This was for the purpose of comparing the sequences, because you cannot compare two DNA sequences between creatures if they are only present in one and not the other. Researchers discovered that many of the short stretches of DNA sequence that code for common proteins were not only highly similar among many types of animals, but nearly identical between humans and other apes.[188]

Before we can explain the true levels of similarity between human and chimp genomes, we need to have a basic understanding of what DNA sequencing actually entails and remove a few myths. While the basic chemical techniques of DNA sequencing did not radically change from the days of its early invention, the use of small-scale robotics and other forms of automation (like those used in factories), began enabling researchers to sequence the small fragments of DNA in massive amounts. Contrary to popular opinion, the DNA of an organism is not sequenced in one big convenient chunk like they show in movies. As Dr. Wile explained previously, it is sequenced in millions of small pieces only hundreds of bases in length and then researchers use computers to assemble the small individual pieces into larger fragments based on overlapping sections. In fact, at the time of this chapter, this is still the case and genome sequencing is far from being a perfect science.[189]

Despite the early discoveries of apparently high DNA similarity between humans and chimps, large-scale DNA sequencing projects began to present a different picture. In 2002, a large DNA sequencing lab produced over 3 million bases of chimp DNA sequence in small 50 to 900 base fragments that were obtained randomly from all over the chimp genome.[190] When these were matched onto the human genome using computer software, only two-thirds of the DNA sequences could be lined up onto human DNA. While there were many short stretches of DNA that were very similar to human, this meant that more than 30% of the chimp DNA sequence was not similar to human at all!

In 2005 the first rough draft of the chimpanzee genome was completed by a collaboration of different labs.[191] Because it was only a rough draft, it consisted of thousands of small chunks of DNA sequence, even after the computational assembly. So guess how the researchers put all the individual pieces of the chimp DNA sequence together to form a complete genome? They assumed that humans evolved from a chimp-like ancestor, and used the human genome as a framework to assemble all of the chimp DNA sequence.[192] In fact, one of the main websites for one of the labs that helped assemble the chimp sequence also admitted that they inserted human DNA sequence, including human genes, into the chimp genome–all based on the assumption of evolution. They thought that these human-like sequences were somehow missing in chimp and added them electronically after the fact. In reality, the published structure of the chimp genome is based on the human genome and it contains human sequence, making it look more human than it really is.

And if all this human-chimp genome research is not biased enough, a large 2013 research project sequenced the genomes of a wide variety of chimpanzees, gorillas, and orangutans to test these species for genetic variation. Believing so strongly in evolution as they do, how do you think they organized all their new DNA sequences?[193] If you guessed that they assembled all of these ape genomes using the human genome as a framework, you were right.

So things have not changed much since 2005, even though DNA sequencing technology has become much cheaper and faster. Surprisingly, the lengths of the individual DNA fragments being produced by new technologies are now much shorter because different chemical techniques are being used. This provides much faster results, but they are even more difficult to assemble.

Unfortunately, the research paper describing the draft chimp genome in 2005 avoided the issue of overall average genome similarity with humans by strictly analyzing and discussing the regions of the genomes that were highly similar. This deceptively reinforced the mythical notion of 98% similarity. However, there was enough information presented in the 2005 report that allowed several independent researchers to calculate overall human chimp genome similarities using this data. They came up with estimates of 70 to 80% DNA sequence similarity.[194] Here is why this result is so important. Evolution has a hard enough time explaining how only 2% of 3 billion bases could have evolved in the 6 million years since chimps and humans supposedly shared a common ancestor. They definitely don't want to take on the task of explaining how some 20 to 30% of three billion bases evolved in such a short time!

Thus, reported high levels of human chimp DNA similarity are actually based on specific highly similar regions shared by both humans and chimps and does not include the regions of the genomes that vastly differ. This is called cherry-picking the data to present a false picture that supports the evolutionary paradigm.

Other published research studies done between 2002 and 2006 attempted to evaluate certain isolated regions of the chimp genome and compare them to human also seemed to add support to the evolutionary paradigm. However, in a research study that I recently published, I went back through all of these different evolutionary reports and reinserted the dissimilar DNA sequence data into the analyses that the evolutionists had omitted (where I could determine it).[195] Not surprisingly, the results showed that the real DNA similarities for the regions that were analyzed varied between about 66% and 86%.

One of the main problems with comparing segments of DNA between different organisms that contain regions of strong dissimilarity is that the computer program commonly used (called BLASTN) will stop matching the DNA when it hits regions that are markedly different. These unmatched sections don't even get included in the final results. If they were, then the overall similarity between human and chimp DNA would be much lower. In addition, the settings of the computer program can be changed to reject DNA sequences that are not similar enough for the researcher. The common default setting used by most evolutionary researchers will kick out anything that is less than 95% to 98% similar. This is convenient for cherry-picking the data, but avoids giving the overall big picture of true differences between two DNA sequences.

In 2011, I tested the BLASTN algorithm in a research project where I compared 40,000 chimp DNA sequences that were each about 740 bases long and were already known to be highly similar to human.[196] The parameters that produced the longest matches showed a DNA similarity of only 86%.

So if chimp DNA is so dissimilar to human and the computer software commonly used stops matching after only a few hundred bases, how can we really find out how similar the human and chimp genomes are? In 2013, I published a research study that resolved this problem by slicing up chimp DNA into small fragments that the software's algorithm could optimally match.[197] I did this for all 24 chimp chromosomes and compared them to human's 23. The results showed that the chimp chromosomes were between 69% and 78% similar to human, depending on the chromosome (the Y chromosome was only 43% similar). Overall, the chimp genome was only about 70% similar to human. Of course, this data confirmed the unpopular but obfuscated results found earlier in secular evolutionary publications, but not popularized by the media or the evolutionists themselves. They knew better.

Some science reporters in the standard media outlets still push the 98% DNA similarity talking point, but those among the human-chimp research community promote the idea less often. Now researchers are more honestly saying that the regions of 96% to 98% similarity are derived from isolated areas and that many regions of dramatic difference do exist between the genomes. However, they won't make statements about overall estimates. Is this because they know it would debunk human evolution? Clearly, the 96–98% similarity idea is crumbling in the research community, but the general public still believes it to be true.

According to my own extensive research on this subject, the human and chimpanzee genomes are only about 70% similar overall. However, there are regions of high similarity, mostly due to protein coding genes (described in more detail below). These areas of high similarity actually share only about 86% matching sequence overall when the algorithm that is used to analyze them is set to produce a long sequence match.[198]

Many scientists believe that high DNA similarity is required to make evolution sound more plausible because many of them know about the limits of mutation rates and variability in the genome. The reality that the human and chimp genomes are substantially different completely wrecks this idea. The regions that are very similar can easily be explained by the fact that common elements of genetic code are often found between different organisms–because they code for similar functions. For the same reason that different kinds of craftsmen all use hammers to drive or pry nails, different kinds of creatures use many of the same biochemical tools to perform common and necessary cellular tasks. The genome is a very complex system of genetic codes, and many of these coding themes are repeated in organisms with similar traits and physiologies because the Divine Programmer created them all. Amazingly, this concept is easier to explain to computer programmers and engineers than it is to biologists, who are steeped in the religion of evolution.

Gene Similarities—the Big Picture

What does it really mean when we say two creatures have the same genes? In reality, it means that only a certain part of a gene sequence is shared. The entire gene itself could be only 80% similar while a small part of it might be 98% similar. In fact, in research that I have not published yet, I have found that the similar parts of human genes—the protein coding regions (called exons)—are only about 86% to 87% similar to chimps on average. Much of this is due to the human exon sequence completely missing in chimps.

One thing that is also important to keep in mind is that our concept of a gene is rapidly changing. The original definition of a gene describes it as a section of DNA that produces a messenger RNA that codes for a protein. It was originally estimated that humans contained about 21,500 to 25,000 of these protein-coding genes. The most recent estimates put this number at about 28,000 to 30,000.[199] Because each of these protein-coding genes produces many different individual messenger RNA variants due to the complexity of gene regulation, over a million different types of proteins can be made from 30,000, or less genes! Nevertheless, less than 5% of the human genome contains actual "exon" protein-coding sequence.

The Myth of "Junk" DNA

Because evolutionary scientists did not know what the other 95% of the genome was doing, and because they needed raw genetic material for evolution to tinker with over millions of years, they labeled it as "junk DNA." However, the concept of junk DNA recently hit the trash. New research from different labs all over the world shows that over 90% of the entire human genome is copied (transcribed) into a dizzying array of RNA molecules that perform many different functions in the cell.[200] This phenomenon, called "pervasive transcription," was discovered in an offshoot of the human genome project called ENCODE, which stands for ENCyclopedia of DNA Elements.[201]

While refuting "junk" DNA, the ENCODE project has also completely redefined our concept of a gene. At the time of this writing, it is estimated that non-protein-coding RNA genes (called long noncoding RNAs) outnumber protein coding genes at least 2 to 1.[202] These long noncoding RNAs (lncRNAs) have similar DNA structures and control features as protein-coding genes, but instead produce functional RNA molecules that do all sorts of things in the cell. Some regulate the function of protein coding genes in various ways and stay in the cell nucleus where the chromosomes are located, while others go into the cell cytoplasm and help regulate different types of processes in collaboration with proteins. Others are even exported out of the cell and used to communicate with other cells. Many of these lncRNA genes play important roles in a process called epigenetics that regulates all aspects of how chromosomes are organized and the genome functions. Now does that sound like junk?

As mentioned earlier, I am currently involved in a research project comparing just the protein coding regions of the human genome to the chimp genome, arguably the most similar segments. I am also comparing the regions of the human genome that encode lncRNAs, because these have been found to be the most specific to a type of organism in all types of animals tested so far.[203] In contrast to many evolutionary studies that compared only the highly similar protein-coding regions of the genome, the lncRNA regions are about 67 to 76% similar—about 10 to 20% less identical than the protein-coding regions.

Clearly, the *whole genome* is a complete storehouse of important information, and textbooks may not catch up to this idea for many years. Using an analogy of a construction project, the protein coding genes are like building blocks and the noncoding regions regulate and determine how the building blocks are used. This is why the protein coding regions tend to be more similar between organisms and the noncoding regions are more dissimilar. Proteins code for skin, hair, hearts, and brains, but noncoding regions help organize these components into the different but distinct arrangements that define each creature. Given this, it is not surprising how humans and chimps are so markedly different!

Chromosome Fusion Debunked

One of the main arguments that human evolutionists have used to support their human chimp story is the supposed fusion of two ape-like chromosomes to form human chromosome number two. The great apes actually contain two more diploid chromosomes than humans–humans have 46 and apes have 48. Because large portions of two small ape chromosomes contain similar banding patterns to human chromosome 2 (although not completely similar) when observed under a microscope, it was believed that they fused during human evolution.[204] Supposedly, the chimp's chromosomes still look like the imaginary ape-human ancestors' did. Thus, these two chimp chromosomes are called 2A and 2B. Gorillas and orangutans also have a 2A and 2B chromosome like chimps.

In 1991, scientists found a short segment of DNA on human chromosome 2 that they claimed was evidence for fusion, even though it was not what they expected based on the analysis of known fusions in living mammals.[205] The alleged fusion sequence consisted of what looked like a degraded head-to-head fusion of chromosome ends (called telomeres) which contain repeats of the DNA sequence TTAGG over and over for thousands of bases. Human telomeres are typically 5,000 to 15,000 bases in length and if these actually fused then you would expect a signature thousands of bases in length.[206] The alleged fusion site, however, is only about 800 bases long and only 70% similar to what would be expected. Plus, a mythical telomere-telomere fusion never has been observed in nature!

This fusion idea, has for many years been masquerading as a knock-down argument proving human evolution from a chimp-like ancestor, but has now been completely debunked. It turns out the alleged fusion site is actually a *functional* DNA sequence inside an important noncoding RNA gene.[207] In 2002, researchers sequenced over 614,000 bases of DNA surrounding the fusion site and found that it was in a gene-rich region. Also, the fusion site itself was inside what they originally labeled a pseudogene (an alleged "dysfunctional relative" of a protein-coding gene).[208] However, new research using data from the ENCODE project now shows that the so-called "fusion site" is part of a noncoding RNA gene that is expressed in many different types of human cells. The research also shows that the alleged fusion site encodes a location inside the gene that binds to proteins that regulate the expression of the gene. What's even more exciting is the fact that none of the other genes within 614,000 bases surrounding the alleged fusion site are found in chimpanzees. They are uniquely human. The fusion is now a debunked myth, although many ignorant evolutionists still attempt to promote it.

Beta-globin Pseudogene Debunked

Another favorite myth that evolutionists like to use to promote human-ape ancestry is the idea of shared mistakes in supposedly broken genes, called pseudogenes. The story they have been telling for at least a decade now is that the ape ancestor's genes were first mutated. Then, after its descendants diverged, both its chimp and human descendant genomes still have those old mutations. After all, they argue, how else could two different but similar species have the same mutations in the same genes unless they evolved from the same ancestor? If this story were true, how would it affect biblical history? Obviously, if we evolved from apes then we were not created in God's image like Scripture says. Accepting these scientist's story would force us to reject God's word. Fortunately, exciting new research shows why we don't have to reject Scripture or science. Now it is being shown that many so-called "pseudogenes" are actually *functional*. They produce important noncoding RNAs that we talked about previously.[209] This means that the shared DNA sequence "mistakes" were actually purposefully created DNA sequences all along.

One example was the beta-globin pseudogene, actually a real gene in the middle of a cluster of five other genes. The other five code for and produce functional proteins. Evolutionists originally claimed that the beta-globin pseudogene was broken because it did not produce a protein and because of its DNA similarity to chimps and other apes. Now multiple studies have shown that it produces long noncoding RNAs and is the most genetically networked gene in the whole beta-globin gene cluster.[210] Genes do not act alone, but are connected in their function to many other genes in the genome, like computer servers are connected to each other to make the internet. Not only do other genes depend on the proper function of the beta-globin pseudogene, but over 250 different types of human cells actively use the gene. Not bad for what is supposed to be a "pseudogene."

GULO Pseudogene Debunked

Another case of so-called evidence for evolution is the GULO pseudogene, which actually looks like a truly broken gene. In animals that have a functional GULO gene, an enzyme is produced that helps make vitamin C. Evolutionists have claimed that humans, chimps and other apes share

GULO genes that mutated in the same places because the mutations occurred in their common ancestor.

However, broken GULO pseudogenes are also found in mice, rats, bats, birds, pigs, and famously, guinea pigs. Did we evolve from guinea pigs? Instead, it looks like this gene may be predisposed to being broken, or mutated, no matter what creature has it. Since humans and other animals can get vitamin C from their diet, they can survive without the gene. Also, the other genes in the GULO biochemical pathway produce proteins that are involved in other important cellular processes. Losing them could be disastrous to the organism. So basically, creatures and man can tolerate having a broken GULO gene by eating vegetables with vitamin C.

In addition, the GULO gene was recently analyzed in its entirety, where researchers found no pattern of common ancestry in it.[211] The GULO gene region and the mutational events that wrecked it are associated with unique categories of a group of DNA features called transposable elements. There are many different types of transposable elements in the human genome which do important things, and their signatures are very distinct. Sometimes they can disrupt genes. In the case of GULO, the transposable element patterns are different and unique in humans and each of the other ape kinds that were evaluated. Therefore, there is no pattern of common ancestry found for GULO among humans and apes—negating this evolutionary argument. Like the claims of 99% similarity, chromosome fusion, and Beta-globin, evolutionists built the GULO argument based on a prior belief in evolution, plus a lack of knowledge about how this biology actually works in cells.

In reality, the GULO pseudogene data utterly defies evolution and vindicates the creation model that predicts genome degradation from an originally created pristine state. This process of genetic decay is found all over the animal kingdom and is called genetic entropy. Cornell University Geneticist

John Sanford has shown in several studies that the human genome is actually in a state of irreversible degeneration, not evolving and getting better.[212] Perhaps Adam and Eve had a working GULO gene and were thus able to manufacture vitamin C whenever their bodies needed it. Today, without vitamin C in our diets, we get the disease called scurvy.

The Human-Chimp Evolution Magic Act

Stage magicians, otherwise known as illusionists, practice their trade by getting you to focus on some aspect of the magician's act to divert your focus from what is really going on or what the other hand is doing. By doing this, they get you to believe something that really isn't true and thus create an illusion—a fake reality. The human-chimp DNA similarity "research" works almost the same way.

The evolutionist who promotes the fake paradigm of human-chimp DNA similarity accomplishes the magic act by getting you to focus on a small set of data representing bits and pieces of hand-picked evidence. This way, you don't see the mountains of hard data utterly defying evolution. While some parts of the human and chimpanzee genomes are very similar—those that the evolutionists focus on—the genomes overall vastly differ, and the hard scientific evidence now proves it. The magic act isn't working any longer, and more and more open-minded scientists are beginning to realize it.

Confronting Human-Chimp Propaganda

To close this chapter, let's discuss a hypothetical exchange that could take place using the information given in this chapter with some human-chimp similarity proponent. This exchange could be with a teacher or maybe a friend or schoolmate. First, the person makes the claim that "humans and chimps are genetically 98–99% identical or similar in their DNA." You can say, "Well that's only partially true for the highly similar regions that have been compared between humans and chimps." You then clarify this response by saying "recent research has actually shown that overall, the genomes are only about 70% similar on average when you include all the DNA." You can also add, "Several thousand genes unique to humans are completely missing in chimps, and scientists have found many genes unique to chimps that are missing in humans." Then ask, "How can you explain these massive differences with evolutionary processes?" In sum, ask, "How is it that such supposedly minor differences in DNA can account for such major and obvious differences between humans and chimps?"

At this point in the conversation, you will rapidly find out if the person is really interested in learning more about the issue of human origins or if they are so zealous about evolutionary beliefs that they won't really be persuaded by any amount of evidence. In reality, the whole modern research field of genetics and genomics is the worst enemy of evolution. As new genomes are being sequenced from different kinds of organisms, they are all appearing as unique sets of DNA containing many genes and other sequences that are specific to that type of creature. Evolutionists call these new creature-specific genes "orphan genes" because they are not found in any other type of creature.[213] Orphan genes appear suddenly in the pattern of life as unique sections of genetic code with no evolutionary history or explanation. Of course, believers in an Omnipotent Creator know that each different genome, such as that for humans and that of chimpanzees, was separately, uniquely, and masterfully engineered at the beginning of creation. God created and embedded each creature's orphan genes to network with all the rest of that creature's genetic coding instructions. The scientific data overwhelmingly suggests that God deserves all the credit, and evolution deserves none.

Chapter 9:

Vestigial Structures

Jerry Bergman, Ph.D.

Why is this Chapter Important?

Most people have heard the common assertion that human bodies have some parts that are "leftover" from the evolutionary process that took "millions of years." Body parts such as the tailbone, tonsils, and the appendix are commonly placed in this category of "extra" or "unnecessary" body parts.

While many evolutionists are just fine with this assumption, many Christian's might ask, "Why would God—who is able to design humans in a complete and perfect fashion—leave such 'extra' or 'unnecessary' parts?" This question is answered by this Chapter by explaining that these supposedly "extra" parts are not extra at all. We do this by providing current medical research that demonstrates just how intentional God was when He designed the human body.

Introduction

One major supposed proof of evolution is the observation that some organs appear to be degenerate or useless, often called vestigial organs. As Professor Senter opines, the "existence of vestigial structures is one of the main lines of evidence for macroevolution."[214] Vestigial organs are usually defined as body structures that were believed to have served some function in an organism's evolutionary history, but are now no longer functional, or close to functionless.[215]

Thus, evolutionists teach that "living creatures, including man, are *virtual museums of structures that have no useful function*, but which represent the remains of organs that once had some use"[216] (emphasis added). Because all of the claimed vestigial organs have now actually been shown to be useful and integral to human function, evolutionists who attempt to salvage their idea have tried to shift gears. They now suggest that some organs have "reduced function," compared to their function in some undefined past. Thus, a new definition for "vestigial" is being used by some evolutionists. A problem with the revisionist definition is: Just how much reduction is required before the "vestigial" label is appropriate? Is 30% a large enough reduction, or will a 10% reduction suffice? In addition, there are so many putative examples of "reduced size" functional structures that the label "vestigial" becomes meaningless.

For example, an analysis of skull shapes of our supposed evolutionary ancestors shows that our human jaw is vestigial compared to our alleged ancestors, since it is claimed to be much smaller in humans today (and also has a reduced function relative to its strength and ability to chew food).[217] Furthermore, not only the human jaw and nose, but our eyes, eyebrows, front limbs, ears, and even our mouth could also be labeled vestigial when compared to our alleged ancestors. For this reason, the term becomes meaningless when defined in this fashion. Anything could be "vestigial" if it simply suits the writer.

Darwin discussed this topic extensively, concluding that vestigial organs speak "infallibly" to evolution.[218] Darwin asserted that the existence of vestigial organs is strong evidence against creation, arguing that vestigial organs are so "extremely common" and "far from presenting a strange difficulty, as they assuredly do on the old doctrine of creation, might even have been anticipated in accordance with evolution."[219]

The view that vestigial organs are critical evidence for macroevolution was further developed by the German anatomist Wiedersheim, who made it his life's work.[220] Wiedersheim compiled a list of over 100 vestigial and so-called "retrogressive structures" that occur in humans. His list included the integument (skin), skeleton, muscles, nervous system, sense organs, digestive, respiratory, circulatory and urogenital systems.[221] Most of these remnants of (past physical) structures are found completely developed in other vertebrate groups.[222] Therefore, Wiedersheim concluded that the "doctrine of special creation or ... any teleological hypothesis" fails to explain these organs.[223]

For the medically-informed reader, we left most of the technical language in this chapter in-tact. Readers without this background, however, should still be able to read this chapter and gain an understanding that God has an incredible design for each and every part of the human body!

Vestigial Problems in Your Textbook

Let us now examine the most common vestigial organ claims. We hope your appreciation grows for God Who did in fact know what He was doing when He *created us in His image* (Genesis 1:27) and Who ensured we are *fearfully and wonderfully made* (Psalm 139:14).

The Coccyx (tailbone)

Humans lack a tail. All lower primates have tails and the human coccyx (tailbone) is interpreted by Darwinists as a rudimentary tail left over from our distant monkey-like ancestors that supposedly had tails. Specifically, Darwin claimed that the "coccyx in man, though functionless as a tail, plainly represents this part in other vertebrate animals."[224]

A major problem with the conclusion that the coccyx shows evolution is that our supposed "nearest relatives" including chimpanzees, gorillas, orangutans, bonobos, gibbons or the lesser apes such as siamangs all lack tails! Only a few of the over 100 types of monkeys and apes, such as spider monkeys, have tails. The primates that have tails tend to be the small cat-like lemurs and tarsiers.

In fact, the coccyx "is merely the terminal portion of the backbone. After all, it does have to have an end!"[225] The major function of the coccyx is an attachment site for the interconnected muscle fibers and tissues that support the bladder neck, urethra, uterus, rectum, and a set of structures that form a bowl-shaped muscular floor, collectively called the pelvic diaphragm, that supports digestive and other internal organs.[226]

The muscles and ligaments that join to the coccyx include the coccygeus muscle ventrally, and the gluteus maximus muscle dorsally. The coccygeus muscles enclose the back part of the pelvis outlet.[227] The levator ani muscles constrict the lower end of both the rectum and vagina, drawing the rectum both forward and upward.[228] The cocygeus muscle, which is inserted into the margin of the coccyx and into the side of the last section of the sacrum, helps to support the posterior organs of the pelvic floor. The coccygeus muscle is a strong, yet flexible, muscle, often described as a "hammock," that adds support to the pelvic diaphragm against abdominal pressure. The coccyx muscle system expands and contracts during urination and bowel movements, and also distends to help enlarge the birth canal during childbirth.[229]

Another useful structure connected to the coccyx is the anococcygeal raphe, a narrow fibrous band that extends from the coccyx to the margin of the anus.[230] Without the coccyx and its attached muscle system, humans would need a very different support system for their internal organs requiring numerous design changes in the human posterior.[231] Darwin was clearly wrong about the coccyx, and it is way past time that textbooks reflect known science about the well-designed end of the human spine.

The Tonsils and Adenoids

Among the organs long considered vestigial are the tonsils and adenoids. The tonsils are three sets of lymph tissues. The first, called palatine tonsils or "the tonsils," consist of two oval masses of lymph tissue (defined below) attached to the side wall at the back of the mouth. The second pair is the nasopharyngeal tonsils, commonly called the adenoids. The last section contains the lingual tonsils, which consist of two masses of lymph tissue located on the dorsum of the tongue.The assumption that the tonsils are vestigial has been one reason for the high frequency of tonsillectomies in the past. Decades ago J. D. Ratcliff wrote that "physicians once thought tonsils were simply useless evolutionary leftovers and took them out thinking that it could do no harm. Today there is considerable evidence that there are more troubles of the respiratory tract after tonsil removal than before, and *doctors generally agree that simple enlargement of tonsils is hardly an indication for surgery*"[232] (emphasis added).

In recent years, researchers have demonstrated the important functions of both the tonsils and adenoids. As a result, most doctors are now reluctant to remove either the tonsils or the adenoids. Medical authorities now actively discourage tonsillectomies.[233]

The tonsils are lymph glands. They help establish the body's defense mechanism that produces disease-fighting antibodies. These defense mechanisms develop during childhood, as children sample and record materials through their mouths. The tonsils begin to shrink in the preteen years to almost nothing in adults, and other organs take over this defense function.[234] Because tonsils are larger in children than in adults, the tonsils are important in the development of the entire immune system.[235] For example, one doctor concluded that:

> The location of the tonsils and adenoids allows them to act as a trap and first line of defense against inhaled or ingested bacteria and viruses. The tonsils and adenoids are made up of lymphoid tissue which manufactures antibodies against invading diseases. Therefore, unless there is an important and specific reason to have the operation, it is better to leave the tonsils and adenoids in place. [236]

The tonsils are continually exposed to the bacteria in air we breathe and for this reason can readily become infected. As part of the body's lymphatic system, they function to fight disease organisms.[237] The tonsils "form a ring of lymphoid tissue" that guards the "entrance of the alimentary [digestive] and respiratory tracts from bacterial invasion." Called "super lymph nodes" they provide first-line defense against bacteria and viruses that cause both sore throats and colds.[238] Although removal of tonsils obviously eliminates tonsillitis (inflammation of the tonsils), it may increase the incidence of strep throat, Hodgkin's disease, and possibly polio.[239] Empirical research on the value of tonsillectomies in preventing infection demonstrate that the "tonsillectomy is of little benefit after the age of eight when the child's natural defenses have already made him immune to many infections." [240]

Just like calling the coccyx a useless evolutionary leftover, calling tonsils useless vestiges of organs that were only useful in our supposed distant evolutionary ancestor's bodies totally ignores the facts. These organs are well-designed and useful, just as if God created them on purpose.

The Vermiform Appendix

The appendix was one of the "strongest evidences" used by Darwin to disprove creationism in his *The Descent of Man* (1871) book: "in consequence of changed diet or habits, the caecum had become much shortened in various animals, the vermiform appendage [appendix] being left as a rudiment of the shortened part... Not only is it useless, but it is sometimes the cause of death ... due to small hard bodies, such as seeds, entering the passage and causing inflammation." [241] Since Darwin, this claim has been repeated often in books and journals. The appendix was once commonly cited in many biology texts as the best example of a vestigial organ. [242]

The human appendix is a small, narrow, worm-shaped tube that varies in length from 1 to 10 inches.[243] Its average length is slightly over three inches long, and less than 1/2 inch wide.[244] The small intestine empties into the large intestine above the floor of the cecum at an entrance passage controlled by a valve. The lower right end of the large intestine in humans terminates somewhat abruptly at an area termed the cecum. The vermiform appendix is connected to the lower part of the cecum.

The Safe House Role

Most bacteria in a healthy human are beneficial and serve several functions, such as to help digest food. If the intestinal bacteria are purged, one function of the appendix is to replenish the digestive system with beneficial bacteria. Its location—just below the normal one-way flow of food and germs in the large intestine in a sort of gut cul-de-sac—supports the safe house role by protecting and fostering the growth of "good germs" needed for various uses in the intestines, and enabling the digestive bacteria system to "reboot" after bouts of disease such as cholera, or the use of antibiotics. Diarrhea is designed to flush out all bacteria from the colon, both good and bad. The bacteria in the appendix are not affected by diarrhea and can rapidly repopulate the colon to quickly reestablish healthy digestion.

For years, we noticed few effects of removing the appendix. Evolutionists thought that if people don't need them, they must be useless. And if it's useless, then it must be a remnant of some evolutionary ancestor that did need it for something. But just because removing a body part does not immediately kill you does not mean that it has no use. One can lose the end of some fingers and still do almost everything that fully fingered people do, but fingertips are still useful. Like fingertips, tonsils and the appendix are useful and, as far as is known, they always have been ever since God created them.

The Functions of the Appendix in Development

The appendix is also involved in producing molecules that aid in directing the movement of lymphocytes to other body locations. During the early years of development, the appendix functions as a lymph organ, assisting with the maturation of B lymphocytes and in the production of immunoglobulin A (IgA) antibodies. Lymph tissue begins to accumulate in the appendix soon after birth and reaches a peak between the second and third decades of life. It decreases rapidly thereafter, practically disappearing after the age of about 60.

The appendix functions to expose white blood cells to the wide variety of antigens normally present in the gastrointestinal tract. Thus, like the thymus, the appendix helps suppress potentially destructive blood- and lymph-borne antibody responses while also promoting local immunity.[245]

In summary, researchers have concluded, "Long thought to be an evolutionary remnant of little significance to normal physiology, the appendix has ... been identified as an important component of mammalian mucosal immune function, particularly B lymphocyte-mediated immune responses and extrathymically derived T lymphocytes."[246] Calling the appendix "vestigial" is a big mistake.

The Thyroid

The thyroid is a two-lobed gland connected by a narrow strip located just below the voice box.[247] German Darwinist Ernst Haeckel long ago asserted that not only is the thyroid vestigial, but that our body contains "many rudimentary organs.... I will only cite the remarkable thyroid gland (thyreoidea)."[248] Because surgeons found that adults could survive after having their thyroid removed, it was assumed by some that it was useless. Wiedersheim listed the thyroid as vestigial because of the "manner in which the thyroid originates."[249] Were they right? Modern medicine has revealed enough about the thyroid for us to find out.

The thyroid is one of the largest endocrine glands, and can grow to as large as 20 grams in adults. The three most important hormones it produces are triiodothyronine (T3) and thyroxine (T4), both of which regulate metabolism, and calcitonin, which regulates calcium levels. Both T3 and T4 stimulate the mitochondria to provide more energy for the body and increase protein synthesis. Without T3 and T4, humans become sluggish, and growth stops. An oversupply (or an undersupply) of thyroxine results in over-activity (or under-activity) of many organs. Defects in this organ at birth can cause a hideous deformity known as cretinism, shown as severe retardation of both physical and mental development.[250] Haeckel was exactly wrong about the Thyroid, but he didn't know its values. Museums and textbook displays still portraying the thyroid as vestigial show an almost criminal disregard of good observational science.

The Thymus

The thymus gland is an example of an important organ that was long judged not only vestigial, but harmful if it became enlarged. Maisel reported that for generations physicians regarded it "as a useless, vestigial organ."[251] Clayton noted that an oversized thymus was once routinely treated with radiation in order to shrink it.[252] Follow-up studies showed that, instead of helping the patient, such radiation treatment caused abnormal growth and a higher level of infectious diseases that persisted longer than normally.

The thymus is a small pinkish-gray body located below the larynx and behind the sternum in the chest.[253] A capsule, from which fingers extend inward, surrounds it and divides it into several small lobes, each of which contains functional units called follicles.

Functions of the Thymus

This once-deemed worthless vestigial structure is now known to be the master gland of the lymphatic system. Without it, the T-cells that protect the body from infection could not function properly because they develop within the thymus gland. Researchers have now solved the thymus enigma, finding that far from being useless, the thymus regulates the intricate immune system which protects us against infectious diseases. Thanks to these discoveries, many researchers are now pursuing new and highly promising lines of attack against a wide range of major diseases, from arthritis to cancer.[254]

The cortex, or outer tissue layer, of the thymus is densely packed with small lymphocytes surrounded by epithelial-reticular cells. The lymphocytes, also called thymic cells, are produced in the cortex and exit the gland through the medulla.[255] The medulla is more vascular than the cortex, and its epithelial-reticular cells outnumber the lymphocytes.

Besides being a master regulator and nursery for disease-fighting T-cells, the thymus takes a dominant role reducing autoimmune problems. These occur where the immune system attacks the person's own cells, called the self-tolerance problem.[256] As research on immune tolerance continues, "the multiplicity of mechanisms protecting the individual from immune responses against self-antigens" and "the critical role the thymus plays is becoming better understood."[257] "Evidence now exists that regulatory cells have a role in preventing reactions against self-antigens, a function as important as their role of clonal deletion of high-affinity self-reactive T-cells."[258]

Regulatory T-cells also help to prevent inappropriate inflammatory responses to non-disease-causing foreign antigens. This system plays an essential role in preventing harmful inflammatory responses to foreign antigens that come in contact with mucous membranes, such as in many allergies.

In summary, a primary function of the thymus is to nurse to maturity small white blood cells called lymphocytes, which are then sent to the spleen and the lymph nodes, where they multiply.[259] There is nothing vestigial about the thymus.

The Pineal Gland

The pineal was first described by French psychiatrist Philip Pineal in the 1790s.[260] The pineal body is a cone-shaped gland positioned deep inside the head, near the brain stem. Scientists are now finding out that the pineal gland's functions include regulating hormones:

> Scientists are closing in on a mystery gland of the human body, the last organ for which no function has been known. It is turning out to be a lively performer with a prominent role in the vital hormone producing endocrine system... Medical science is now finding what nature really intended by placing a pea-sized organ in the middle of the head.[261]

Of course, the Creator really deserves credit for the pineal gland, not nature. Nevertheless, the pineal gland also serves in reproduction:

> It has long been known that reduction in the amount of light reaching the eyes stimulates this small gland to synthesize and secrete an anti-gonadotrophic hormone(s) which results in marked attenuation of virtually all aspects of reproductive physiology.[262]

Researchers at the National Institute of Mental Health found that the pineal gland is a very active member of the body's network of endocrine glands, especially during certain growth stages.

The Pineal Gland and Melatonin Production

The pineal gland's most commonly mentioned function is its role in producing the hormone melatonin.[263] Cells in the pineal gland produce a special enzyme that converts serotonin to melatonin.[264] Melatonin is produced mainly in the pineal gland of vertebrates, but is also produced in a variety of other tissues. [265]

Light-dark levels are communicated to the brain from the retina to the pineal gland and help regulate melatonin levels. Melatonin is also a sleep-inducing hormone. This is why darkness generally promotes sleepiness.[266]

Melatonin also has important immune function stimulatory properties. It enhances the release of T-helper cell type 1 cytokines such as gamma-interferon and IL-2, counteracts stress-induced immunodepression and other secondary immunodeficiencies, protects against lethal viral encephalitis, bacterial diseases, and septic shock, and diminishes toxicity associated with several common chemotherapeutic agents.[267] The administration of melatonin also increases thymus cellularity and antibody responses.[268] Conversely, pinealectomy accelerates both thymic involution and depresses the humeral and cell-mediated immune response.[269]

Pineal and Reproduction

The pineal gland is the primary controller of the timing of the onset of puberty, a critical developmental function. Melatonin regulates the production of anti-gonadotropin hormones. These help block the effects of hormones that stimulate gonad development. Damage to the pineal gland leads to early puberty in males. Conversely, if the pineal gland is overactive, puberty is delayed. Among melatonin's many other reproductive functions is regulation of the estrus cycle in women. Melatonin levels decrease as women age, particularly after they pass child-bearing age.[270] Changes in melatonin levels may be responsible for some sleep difficulties in menopausal females.

Before the advent of modern artificial lighting, the number of hours humans spent in darkness was much greater. Today, bright lighting found in almost all homes and offices may be affecting our reproductive cycle. Exposure to a large amount of light during most of one's waking hours may cause the onset of sexual maturity at an earlier age, and even the higher rate of multiple births.

Studies on "pre-electric" Inuit Indians support the conclusion that light and the pineal gland are important in reproduction. When it is dark for months at a time in their arctic home, Inuit women stop producing eggs altogether and men become less sexually active. When daylight returns, both the women and the men resume their "normal" reproductive cycles.[271]

The "Nictitating Membrane" in the Human Eye

An excellent example of another commonly mislabeled vestigial organ is the so-called nictitating membrane remnant in the human eye. A nictitating membrane, or "third eyelid," is a very thin and transparent structure that small muscles move horizontally across the eye surface to clean and moisten the eye while maintaining sight. It hinges at the inner side of the lower eyelid of many animals. To nictitate means to move rapidly back and forth over the front of the eye.[272] The nictitating membrane is especially important in animals that live in certain environments, such as those that are exposed to dust and dirt like birds, reptiles, and mammals, or marine animals such as fish. Charles Darwin wrote about the "nictitating membrane:"

> ...with its accessory muscles and other structures, is especially well developed in birds, and is of much functional importance to them, as it can be rapidly drawn across the whole eye-ball. It is found in some reptiles and amphibians, and in certain fishes, as in sharks. ... But in man, the quadrumana, and most other mammals, it exists, as is admitted by all anatomists, as a mere rudiment, called the semilunar fold.[273]

Many continue to repeat Darwin's wrong idea about this membrane being a vestigial structure, even though, as we will show, it is clearly important in the human eye.[274]

Its Use in Humans

The classic eye anatomy textbook by Snell and Lemp accurately describes what we now recognize as the misnamed nictitating membrane. The plica semiluminaris, or "plica" for short, is a semilunar fold located on the inner corner of the eye to allow that side of the human eyeball to move further inward, toward the nose.[275] Its anatomy reveals a delicate half-moon-shaped vertical fold. The eye has about 50–55% rotation, but without the plica semilunaris, the rotation would be much less. There exists slack that must be taken up when the eye looks forward or side-to-side; hence the fold. No such arrangement exists for looking up or down, for at this area the fornix is very deep. The absence of a deep medial fornix is required for the puncta to dip into superficial strips of tear fluid.[276] Because the plica allows generous eye rotation, it actually is an example of over-design. [277]

Another function of the plica semilunaris is to collect foreign material that sticks to the eyeball. Stibbe notes on a windy day the eyes can rapidly accumulate dust, but due to the plica they can usually effectively remove it.[278] To do this, it secretes a thick sticky fatty liquid that effectively collects foreign material and, in essence, insulates the material for easy removal from the eye without fear of scratching or damaging the delicate eye surface. The critical role of the plica in clearing foreign objects from the eye surface has been recognized since at least 1927. This should be an embarrassment to those who have thought of it as vestigial since then.

Muscle and Bone Variations as Vestigial Organs

Most of the over 100 vestigial organs and structures listed in Wiedersheim's original 1895 work were small muscles or minor variations in bones, and not glands or discreet organs such as the human appendix.[279] Many of these muscles were labeled vestigial because they were small and made only a small contribution, or supposedly no contribution, to the total muscle force. The problem is, if a muscle is vestigial it would rapidly shrink, as research on living in a weightless situation, such as in outer space, has documented.

Thus, if a muscle has not atrophied it must be functional. It is now known that most small, short body muscles produce fine adjustments in the movement of larger muscles, or serve other roles, such as in proprioception.[280] The proprioceptive system allows the body to rapidly and accurately control limb position. It is why falling cats so often land on their feet. Anatomist David Menton concludes that:

> ...most muscles have a sensory function in addition to their more obvious motor function. ...that some of the smaller muscles in our body that were once considered vestigial, on the basis of their small size and weak contractile strength, are in fact sensory organs rather than motor organs.[281]

Certain other muscles and bone variations are also labeled vestigial primarily because they are not present in most (or many) people and are not required for survival. As is clearly evident in human skill differences, these muscle variations help to produce the enormous variety in many abilities so evident in modern humans. An example is the gross body muscle development of the stereotyped computer programmer compared with a football player. More commonly, many muscles are not well developed in most persons today in Western society due to our sedentary lifestyle.

This does not mean that they are vestigial, but only demonstrates their lack of use in modern life. It also demonstrates a very different lifestyle today than in the past. Lifestyle differences could cause many of these "less developed" muscles to be much larger. Would evolutionists have called them vestigial if they saw how much larger they were in a more athletic person's body? The fact that some individuals are superior athletes from a young age is evidence that genetic components clearly play an important role in complex physical activities. DeVries maintains that athletic ability depends on variations of numerous aspects of muscle cell structure and physiology.[282] Certain muscles and muscle types must first be present before they can ever be developed by proper training.

Gifted athletes, such as gymnastic and acrobatic stars, may tend to have certain muscles that some people may not even possess, or they can develop certain muscles to a greater extent. Most human abilities appear to be influenced by genetic differences that result from body structure variations. It follows that the human muscle system would likewise be influenced by heredity.

The argument that some small muscle is vestigial depends heavily on judgments as to the value and the individual use of a particular structure. It is clear that none of the so-called vestigial muscles are in any way harmful. Indeed, if they are developed at all, then those who have them may enjoy an advantage in certain activities, even if it is only an athletic or aesthetic advantage.

Scientist have clearly identified specific and well-designed purposes for every single supposedly vestigial organ so far proposed. Darwinist books, movies, and displays are dead wrong if they promote the concept of vestigial organs, which don't actually exist.

Conclusion

If the God of the Bible is true, we would expect to find clear "evidence trails" described in each chapter:

- Chapter 1 (Can We Trust the Bible?): We would expect to find *inspired content* that withstands time; prophecies that are foretold centuries before they come true; and a consistent description of intelligent design and scientific underpinnings of Creation.
- Chapter 2 (Did Noah's Flood Really Happen?): We would expect to find billions of dead things laid down by water all over the earth, including the high mountains and major "bonebeds" where thousands of mixed and same-species animals are jumbled together, buried by the deluge of the flood; major coal deposits from countless buried forests and animals; evidence of mountain formations made by buckling as the continents shifted catastrophically; and a God-designed Ark that was built to weather the worst storm in history, filled with a feasible number of "kinds" necessary to repopulate the Earth with the animals we see today.
- Chapter 3 (The Age of the Earth, Dating Methods, and Evolution): We would expect to find evidences that disprove "old-age" dating methods and evolutionary "gradualism" assumptions that cannot be relied upon;

evidence of young coal deposits; "young" diamonds; and numerous cases of "young bones and flesh" in supposedly old Earth matter; and young ocean.

- Chapter 4 (Do Fossils Show Evolution?): We would expect to find that evolutionary "ancestral forms," "transitional forms," and "divergent forms" never existed; that the fossil evidence does not allow for gradualism; and that Noah's Flood provides the most reasonable and logical explanation for the billions of dead animals in Earth's crust all over the world.
- Chapter 5 (Do Fossils of Early Man Prove Evolution?): We would expect to find that men and women are uniquely and intentionally designed by a Creator and that the supposed "early man" fossils are either misidentified mammals, wholly human, deliberate deceptions, or unidentified.
- Chapter 6 (Natural Selection and Evolution): We would expect to find that "Darwin's Finches" are great examples of God-designed adaptation (but not evolution) and that God has a Divine formula for life.
- Chapter 7 (Did Hippos Evolve into Whales?): We would expect to find that several mammal and whale designs died off during the Flood and that several "created kinds" still exist today in the perfectly-designed form necessary for navigating and living in the ocean.
- Chapter 8 (Are Humans and Chimps Really 99% Similar?): We would expect to find, at very intuitive as well as advanced scientific levels, that humans and chimps are distinctly different "kinds," even though they share some common building blocks used by God in their design.
- Chapter 9 (Vestigial Structures): We would expect to find that virtually every square inch of the human

> body is necessary and shouts "grand design" from the beginning of Creation.

In this book we have tried to refute what students informed us were the most convincing arguments for evolution from their biology and earth science textbooks. We hope you noticed that we squarely faced the best that evolutionary-based science offers, and demonstrated how textbooks sometimes use wrong history and inaccurate science.

In many instances, Christians *should* trust science textbooks and the scientific method. Indeed, science has advanced medicine, space exploration, and technology beyond what we could have even imagined one hundred years ago. Thus, science applied in the present can advance so many fields into the future.

But what about the past? How accurately can scientific methods take us into the past? Certainly, in fields like crime scene investigation, scientists have developed very reliable methods for determining when certain events happened, what elements were involved, and other factors. But what about hundreds or even thousands of years ago, when present scientists did not exist? Can we reliably use scientific tools for knowing, for certain, when major events occurred, such as the dinosaurs going extinct some 65 million years ago as evolutionist claim? That's certainly a long time ago to make such a projection—especially by using the supposed age of the rocks to date the fossils.

Put simply, textbooks are often wrong. The largest errors occur where textbook authors and the scientific works that they cite make historical statements. You can easily recognize these by their use of past tense verbs. Whenever you see a past-tense assertion like "The Earth formed 4.6 billion years ago," just ask, "How do they know?"

Often, they have no idea—they just trust that whoever told them does know. In truth, the teller was probably thinking the same thing. When we see past tenses, we can also ask, "Were they there to witness the events they portray?" or, "Is that even a scientific (experiment-based) claim?" If not, then we have strong reasons to suspect that their assertions masquerade as science when in fact they stem from miracle-ignoring histories.

Textbook authors religiously confine their statements to a secularized history that by definition excludes the Bible—regardless of the evidence. This is exactly the attitude that Peter, carried along by the Holy Spirit as he penned the words, foretold would occur. In 2 Peter 3, he wrote, "For this they willfully forget: that by the word of God the heavens were of old, and the Earth standing out of water and in the water, by which the world that then existed perished, being flooded with water." Peter strongly warned his readers—you and I inside the church—"that scoffers will come in the last days" and would deliberately forget the two great historical miracles: creation and the Flood judgment.

He was concerned that their false teachings would derail untrained Christians. That is exactly our concern, too. So, we wrote this book to help train you how to think biblically and scientifically about origins. If secular textbook authors are some of Peter's foretold scoffers who force God and Genesis out of their minds so they can pretend they will escape the judgment of God, then they merely fulfil this very Scripture. In the end, the Bible is right. We can trust its every word. As Jesus said to our Father, "Your word is truth." (John 17: 17)

Helpful Resources

The following websites are recommended for further research:

- Answers in Genesis: http://www.answersingenesis.com
- Answers in Genesis (High School Biology): http://www.evolutionexposed.com
- Creation Ministries International: http://www.creation.com
- Creation Today: http://www.creationtoday.org/about/eric-hovind/
- Creation Wiki: http://creationwiki.org/
- Evolution: The Grand Experiment with by Dr. Carl Werner: http://www.thegrandexperiment.com/index.html
- Institute for Creation Research: http://www.icr.org
- Josh McDowell Ministry: www.josh.org

Endnotes

[1] Ken Ham, "Culture and Church in Crisis," AnswersinGenesis.com: *http://www.answersingenesis.org/articles/am/v2/n1/culture-church-crisis* (January 1, 2014) and survey data: *http://www.answersingenesis.org/articles/am/v2/n1/aig-poll (data)* (January 1, 2014).

[2] Results for this USA Today/Gallup poll are based on telephone interviews conducted May 10–13, 2012, with a random sample of 1,012 adults, aged 18 and older, living in all 50 U.S. states and the District of Columbia.

[3] Frank Newport, "In U.S., 46% Hold Creationist View of Human Origins: Highly Religious Americans most likely to believe in Creationism," Gallop.com: *http://www.gallup.com/poll/155003/hold-creationist-view-human-origins.aspx* (June 1, 2012).

[4] Kenneth R. Miller & Joseph S. Levine, *Biology* (Boston, Mass: Pearson, 2010): 466.

[5] Introduction and Table from: "The Bible and Science Agree," Creationism.org: *http://www.creationism.org/articles/BibleSci.htm* (January 1, 2014).

[6] Ken Ham & T. Hillard, *Already Gone: Why your Kids will Quit Church and what you can do stop it* (Green Forest, AR: Master Books, 2009).

[7] S. Michael Houdmann, "How and when was the Canon of the Bible put together?" Got Questions Online: *http://www.gotquestions.org/canon-Bible.html* (November 7, 2013).

[8] The reader is encouraged to review these additional resources: Henry Halley, *Halley's Bible Handbook* (Grand Rapids: Zondervan Publishing House, 1927, 1965); Arthur Maxwell, *Your Bible and You* (Washington D.C.: Review and Herald Publishing Association, 1959); Merrill Unger, *Unger's Bible Handbook* (Chicago: Moody Press, 1967).

[9] For example, in 1946 the Dead Sea Scrolls were discovered, which included over 900 manuscripts dating from 408 B.C. to A.D. 318. These manuscripts were written mostly on parchment (made of animal hide) but with some written on papyrus. Because these materials are fragile, they have to be kept behind special glass in climate controlled areas.

[10] Josh McDowell, *The New Evidence that Demands a Verdict* (Nashville: Thomas Nelson Publishers).

[11] McDowell, *The New Evidence that Demands a Verdict*, p.38.

[12] McDowell, *The New Evidence that Demands a Verdict*, p.38.

[13] Most of the 11 verses come from 3 John. See: Norman Geisler & William Nix. *A General Introduction to the Bible* (Chicago: Moody Press, 1986), 430.

[14] Geisler & Nix, *A General Introduction to the Bible*, p. 430.

[15] Theophilus ben Ananus was the High Priest in Jerusalem from A.D. 37 to 41 and was one of the wealthiest and most influential Jewish families in Iudaea Province during the 1st century. He was also the brother-in-law of Joseph Caiaphas, the High Priest before whom Jesus appeared. See Wikipedia and B. Cooper, *The Authenticity of the Book of Genesis* (Portsmouth, UK: Creation Science Movement, 2012).

[16] B. Cooper, *Authenticity of the New Testament, Vol. 1: The Gospels*. Electronic book (2013).

[17] The Digital Dead Sea Scrolls Online, Directory of Qumran Dead Sea Scroll: *http://dss.collections.imj.org.il/isaiah* (December 10, 2013).

[18] Source for DSS: Fred Mille, "Qumran Great Isaiah Scroll," Great Isaiah Scroll: *http://www.moellerhaus.com/qumdir.*

htm; Source for Aleppo Codes JPS: "Mechon Mamre" (Hebrew for Mamre Institute): *http://www.mechon-mamre.org/p/pt/pt1053.htm* (December 10, 2013).

[19] Norman & Nix. *A General Introduction to the Bible*.

[20] Samuel Davidson, *Hebrew Text of the Old Testament*, 2d ed. (London: Samuel Bagster & Sons, 1859), 89.

[21] Mary Fairchild, "44 Prophecies of the Messiah Fulfilled in Jesus Christ," About.com: *http://christianity.about.com/od/biblefactsandlists/a/Prophecies-Jesus.htm* (December 18, 2013).

[22] See: Genesis 7:19 ("all the high hills under the whole heaven were covered"); Genesis 7:21–22 ("all flesh died that moved upon the earth…all that was in the dry land"); Matthew 24:39 ("The flood came, and took them all away"); and 2 Peter 3:6 ("By these waters also the world of that time was deluged and destroyed."). God also promised in Genesis 9:11 that there would be no more floods like the one of Noah's day.

[23] Ken Ham, "They Can't Allow "It"!" AnswersinGenesis.com: *http://www.answersingenesis.org/articles/au/cant-allow-it* (January 1, 2014).

[24] Eva Vergara & Ian James, "Whale Fossil Bonanza in Desert Poses Mystery," Science on msnbc.com: *http://www.msnbc.msn.com/id/45367885/ns/technology_and_science-science/* (November 20, 2013).

[25] D.A. Eberth, D.B. Brinkman, & V. Barkas, "A Centrosaurine Mega-bonebed from the Upper Cretaceous of Southern Alberta: Implications for Behaviour and Death Events" in *New Perspectives on Horned Dinosaurs: The Ceratopsian Symposium at the Royal Tyrrell Museum* (September 2007).

[26] Michael Reilly, "Dinosaurs' Last Stand Found in China?" Discovery.com: *http://news.discovery.com/earth/dinosaurs-last-stand-found-in-china.htm* (January 1, 2014).

[27] Michael J. Oard, "The Extinction of the Dinosaurs," *Journal of Creation* 11(2) (1997): 137–154.

[28] J.R. Horner & J. Gorman, *Digging Dinosaurs* (New York: Workman Publishing, 1988), 122–123.

[29] John Woodmorappe, "The Karoo Vertebrate Non-Problem: 800 Billion Fossils or Not," *CEN Technical Journal* 14, no.2 (2000): 47.

[30] R. Broom, *The Mammal-like Reptiles of South Africa* (London: H.F.G., 1932), 309.

[31] Steven Austin, "Nautiloid Mass Kill and Burial Event, Redwall Limestone (Lower Mississippian) Grand Canyon Region, Arizona and Nevada," in Ivey Jr. (Ed.). *Proceedings of the Fifth International Conference on Creationism* (Pittsburg, Pennsylvania: Creation Science Fellowship): 55–99.

[32] Andrew Snelling, *Earth's Catastrophic Past: Geology, Creation & the Flood*, Vol. 2 (Dallas, TX: Institute for Creation Research, 2009), 537.

[33] Snelling, *Earth's Catastrophic Past: Geology, Creation & the Flood*, p. 537.

[34] David Cloud, *An Unshakeable Faith: A Christian Apologetics Course* (Port Huron, MI: Way of Life Literature, 2011).

[35] Snelling, *Earth's Catastrophic Past: Geology, Creation & the Flood*, p. 538.

[36] Snelling, *Earth's Catastrophic Past: Geology, Creation & the Flood*, p. 539.

[37] Andrew Snelling, "The World's a Graveyard Flood Evidence Number Two," AnswersinGenesis: *http://www.answersingenesis.org/articles/am/v3/n2/world-graveyard* (January 1, 2014).

[38] Cloud, *An Unshakeable Faith: A Christian Apologetics Course*.

[39] Cloud, *An Unshakeable Faith: A Christian Apologetics Course*.

[40] N. O. Newell, "Adequacy of the Fossil Record," *Journal of Paleontology*, 33 (1959): 496.

[41] Darwin, *The Origin of Species*, p. 298.

[42] Luther Sunderland, *Darwin's Enigma* (Arkansas: Master Books, 1998), 129.

[43] Cloud, *An Unshakeable Faith: A Christian Apologetics Course*.

[44] Photo by Ian Juby. Reproduced with permission. Tas Walker, "Polystrate Fossils: Evidence for a Young Earth," Creation.com: *http://creation.com/polystrate-fossils-evidence-for-a-young-earth* (January 3, 2014).

[45] John D. Morris, "What Are Polystrate Fossils?" *Acts & Facts*, 24 (9) (1995).

[46] Tas Walker & Carl Wieland, "Kamikaze ichthyosaur? Long-age Thinking Dealt a Lethal Body Blow," *Creation Magazine*, 27 (4) (September 2005). See: Creation.com: *http://creation.com/kamikaze-ichthyosaur* (December 31, 2013).

[47] Walker & Wieland, 2005 (figure reproduced with permission: Creation.com).

[48] Carl Wieland, *Stones and Bones* (Green Forest, AR: Master Books, 1984).

[49] Andrew Snelling, "Transcontinental Rock Layers: Flood Evidence Number Three," Answers Magazine.com: *http://www.answersingenesis.org/articles/am/v3/n3/transcontinental-rock-layers* (December 17, 2013).

[50] David Catchpoole, "Giant Oysters on the Mountain," *Creation,* 24 (2) (March 2002): 54–55.

[51] Richard F. Flint. *Glacial Geology and the Pleistocene Epoch* (New York: Wiley, 1947), 514–515.

[52] Humans lived much longer before the Flood due to both changes in human DNA (from sin entering the world through the fall of Adam) and climate changes in the post-flood world. See D. Menton & G. Purdom, "Did People Like Adam and Noah Really Live Over 900 Years of Age?" in Ken Ham. *The New Answers Book 2* (Green Forest: AR Master Books), 164; David Menton & Georgia

Purdom, "Chapter 16: Did People Like Adam and Noah Really Live Over 900 Years of Age?" (May 27, 2010). AnswersinGenesis.com: *http://www.answersingenesis.org/articles/nab2/adam-and-noah-live* (January 1, 2014).

[53] There is no conflict regarding the estimated age of these trees and the estimated time of Noah's Flood. See: Mark Matthews, "Evidence for multiple ring growth per year in Bristlecone Pines," *Journal of Creation,* 20 (3) (2006): 95–103.

[54] D.E Kreiss, "Can the Redwoods Date the Flood?" *Institute for Creation Research Impact* (Article #134, 1984).

[55] Michael Oard, "The Remarkable African Planation Surface," *Journal of Creation* 25 (1) (2011): 111–122.

[56] Dr. Hong earned his Ph.D. degree in applied mechanics from the University of Michigan, Ann Arbor.

[57] S.W. Hong, S.S. Na, B.S. Hyun, S.Y. Hong, D.S. Gong, K.J. Kang, S.H. Suh, K.H. Lee, and Y.G. Je, "Safety investigation of Noah's Ark in a seaway," Creation.com: *http://creation.com/safety-investigation-of-noahs-ark-in-a-seaway* (January 1, 2014).

[58] John Whitcomb, *The World that Perished* (Grand Rapids, Michigan: Baker Book House, 1988), 24.

[59] See John Woodmorappe, *Noah's Ark: A Feasibility Study* (Dallas, TX: Institute for Creation Research, 2009).

[60] Woodmorappe, *Noah's Ark: A Feasibility Study*, 2009.

[61] Readers are encouraged to study where the water went after the Flood at the AnswersinGenesis.com website.

[62] Humans lived much longer before the Flood due to both changes in human DNA (from sin entering the world through the fall of Adam) and climate changes in the post-flood world. See D. Menton & G. Purdom, "Did People Like Adam and Noah Really Live Over 900 Years of Age?" in Ken Ham. *The New Answers Book 2* (Green Forest: AR Master Books), 164; David Menton & Georgia Purdom, "Chapter 16: Did People Like Adam and Noah

Really Live Over 900 Years of Age?" (May 27, 2010). AnswersinGenesis.com: *http://www.answersingenesis.org/articles/nab2/adam-and-noah-live* (January 1, 2014).

[63] There are several resources for this topic of study. See, for example: "Michael Oard, "Chapter 7: The Genesis Flood Caused the Ice Age," (October 1, 2004), AnswersinGenesis.com: *http://www.answersingenesis.org/articles/fit/flood-caused-ice-age* (January 6, 2014).

[64] Ken Ham, "What Really Happened to the Dinosaurs?" (October 25, 2007), AnswersinGenesis.com: *http://www.answersingenesis.org/articles/nab/what-happened-to-the-dinosaurs* (January 6, 2014).

[65] Miller & Levine, *Biology,* p. 466.

[66] Gunter Faure, *Principles of Isotope Geology,* 2nd ed. (John Wiley & Sons, 1986), 41, 119, 288.

[67] A.O. Woodford, *Historical Geology* (W.H. Freeman and Company, 1965), 191–220.

[68] Judah Etinger, *Foolish Faith* (Green Forest, AR: Master Books, 2003), Chapter 3.

[69] Larry Vardiman, "The Age of the Earth's Atmosphere, a Study of the Helium Flux through the Atmosphere," *Institute for Creation Research*, 1990.

[70] C.S. Noble & J.J Naughton, *Science*, 162 (1968): 265–266.

[71] Data compiled and modified after Snelling (1998): Andrew Snelling, "The Cause of Anomalous Potassium-Argon "ages" for Recent Andesite Flows at Mt. Ngauruhoe, New Zealand, and the Implications for Potassium-argon Dating," in Robert E. Walsh (ed.), *Proceedings of the Fourth International Conference on Creationism* (1998), 503–525.

[72] J. Hebert, "Rethinking Carbon-14 Dating: What Does It Really Tell Us about the Age of the Earth?" *Acts & Facts* 42 (4) (2013): 12–14.

[73] Modified from: J. Baumgardner, "Carbon-14 Evidence for a Recent Global Flood and a Young Earth." In *Radioisotopes and the Age of the Earth: Results of a*

Young-Earth Creationist Research Initiative. Vardiman, L., A. A. Snelling, and E. F. Chaffin, eds. (San Diego, CA: Institute for Creation Research and Chino Valley, AZ: Creation Research Society), 605 (Table 2).

74 M.J. Walter, S.C. Kohn, D. Araugo, G.P. Bulanova, C.B. Smith, E. Gaillou, J. Wang, A. Steele, S. B., Shirey, "Deep Mantle Cycling of Oceanic Crust: Evidence from Diamonds and Their Mineral Inclusions," *Science*, 334 no. 6052 (September 15, 2011): 54–57.

75 Walter et al., 2011.

76 Modified from Baumgardner, 2005, Table 6, p. 614.

77 Baumgardner, 2005.

78 Brian Thomas, "*The Incredible, Edible '190 Million-Year-Old Egg,'*" Institute for Creation Research Online: *http://www.icr.org/article/7415/*) (December 8, 2013).

79 M.H. Schweitzer, L. Chiappe, A. C. Garrido, J.M. Lowenstein, & S.H. Pincus, "Molecular Preservation in Late Cretaceous Sauropod Dinosaur Eggshells," *Proceedings of the Royal Society B: Biological Sciences*, Volume 272 (1565) (2005): 775–784.

80 Brian Thomas, "Published Reports of Original Soft Tissue Fossils" Institute for Creation Research Online: *http://www.icr.org/soft-tissue-list/* (December 20, 2013).

81 Brian Thomas, "A Review of Original Tissue Fossils and Their Age Implications," in M. Horstemeyer (ed.), *Proceedings of the Seventh International Conference on Creationism* (2013).

82 Data compiled and simplified from Tables 1 and 2 in Austin and Humphries (1990): Stephen Austin & D. Humphreys, Russell, "The Sea's Missing Salt: A Dilemma for Evolutionists," in R. E. Walsh & C. L. Brooks (eds.), *Proceedings of the Fourth International Conference on Creationism* (1990), 17–33.

83 Snelling, *Earth's Catastrophic Past*.

84 Snelling, *Earth's Catastrophic Past*.

[85] Don DeYoung, *Thousands...Not Billions* (Green Forest, AR: Master Books, 2005).

[86] Jonathan Wells, *Icons of Evolution: Science or Myth?—Why Much of What We Teach About Evolution Is Wrong* (Washington, D.C.: Regnery Publishing, Inc., 2000), 35, 37.

[87] The coelacanth is supposedly an ancestor to amphibians that dates back 300 million years; however, the coelacanth appears "suddenly" in the fossil record, and modern coelacanths "were also found to give birth to live young (like some sharks), unlike their supposed descendants, the amphibians." See: K.S. Thomson, *Living Fossil* (New York, NY: W.W. Norton & Company, 1991), 137–144.

[88] Creationwiki.com: *http://creationwiki.org/Archaeopteryx* (January 3, 2014).

[89] Percival Davis, Dean H. Kenyon, & Charles B. Thaxton (ed). *Of Pandas and People: The Central Question of Biological Origins,* 2d ed. (Dallas, TX: Haughton Publishing Company, 1989), 22–23.

[90] John D. Morris, *The Young Earth: The Real History of the Earth, Past, Present, and Future* (Colorado Springs, CO: Master Books, 1994).

[91] Jerry Adler & John Carey, "Is Man a Subtle Accident?" *Newsweek*, 8, no. 95 (Nov. 3, 1980), 96.

[92] Stephen J. Gould & Niles Eldredge, "Punctuated Equilibria: The Tempo and Mode of Evolution Reconsidered," *Paleobiology*, 3, no. 2 (April 1977), 115–151.

[93] Brian Thomas, "150 Years Later, Fossils Still Don't Help Darwin," Institute for Creation Research Online: *http://www.icr.org/article/4546/* (December 20, 2013).

[94] Carl Werner, "Evolution the Grand Experiment," The Grand Experiment: *http://www.thegrandexperiment.com/index.html* (January 1, 2014).

[95] Carl Werner, *Living Fossils. Evolution: The Grand Experiment* (Vol. 2) (Green Forest, AR: New Leaf Press, 2008), 242.

[96] Carl Werner, *Evolution: The Grand Experiment (*Green Forest, AR: New Leaf Press, 2007), 86.

[97] Chart adapted from: Michael Denton, *Evolution: A Theory in Crisis* (Bethesda: Adler & Adler, 1985).

[98] Charles Darwin, *The Origin of Species by Means of Natural Selection* (New York: The Modern Library, 1859), 124-125.

[99] Wells, *Icons of Evolution: Science or Myth?—Why Much of What We Teach About Evolution Is Wrong*, pp. 41–42.

[100] Robert F. DeHaan & John L. Wiester, "*The Cambrian Explosion: The Fossil Record & Intelligent Design,*" *Touchstone (*July/August 1999), 65–69.

[101] Wells, *Icons of Evolution: Science or Myth?—Why Much of What We Teach About Evolution Is Wrong*, 42.

[102] DeHaan & Wiester, 1999, p. 68.

[103] Paul S. Taylor, *The Illustrated ORIGINS Answer Book*, 4th ed. (Mesa, AZ: Eden Productions, 1992), 97.

[104] A fourth category also exists: Those findings that are unknown or unidentified.

[105] William K. Gregory, "Hesperopithecus Apparently Not an Ape nor a Man," *Science*, 66 (1720) (December 16, 1927): 579-581.

[106] Ralph M. Wetzel, et al., "Catagonus, An 'Extinct' Peccary, Alive in Paraguay," *Science*, 189 (4200) (Aug. 1, 1975): 379.

[107] Duane T. Gish, *Evolution: The Fossils Still Say NO!* (El Cajon, CA: Institute for Creation Research, 1995), 328.

[108] Herbert Wray, "Was Lucy a Climber? Dissenting Views of Ancient Bones," *Science News,* 122 (August 21, 1982): 116.

[109] Brian G. Richmond & David S. Strait, "Evidence That Humans Evolved From a Knuckle-Walking Ancestor," *Nature*, 404 (6776) (March 23, 2000), 339–340, 382–385.

[110] Sir Solly Zuckerman, *Beyond the Ivory Tower* (London: Taplinger Publishing Co., 1970), 78.

[111] Wray Herbert, "Lucy's Uncommon Forbear," *Science News*, 123 (February 5, 1983): 89.

[112] Albert W. Mehlert, "Lucy—Evolution's Solitary Claim for an Ape/Man: Her Position is Slipping Away," *Creation Research Society Quarterly*, 22 (3) (December, 1985): 145.

[113] Marvin L. Lubenow, *Bones of Contention* (Grand Rapids, MI: Baker Books, 1992), 179.

[114] DeWitt Steele & Gregory Parker, *Science of the Physical Creation*, 2d ed. (Pensacola, FL: A Beka Book, 1996), 299.

[115] "News to Note" (October 3, 2009). AnswersinGenesis.com: *http://www.answersingenesis.org/articles/2009/10/03/news-to-note-10032009* (January 5, 2014).

[116] B. Asfaw, R.T. Kono, D. Kubo, C.O. Lovejoy, T.D. White, "The Ardipithecus Ramidus Skull and its Implications for Hominid Origins," *Science* 326 (October 2, 2009): 5949.

[117] Brian Thomas, "Did Humans Evolve from 'Ardi'"? Acts and Facts (October 6, 2009), ICR.com: *http://www.icr.org/article/4982/* (January 6, 2014).

[118] Kate Wong, "Weak Link: Fossil Darwinius Has Its 15 Minutes: Skepticism about a fossil cast as a missing link in human ancestry," Scientific American: *http://www.scientificamerican.com/article.cfm?id=weak-link-fossil-darwinius* (January 6, 2014).

[119] National Geographic News, "Missing Link Found: New Fossil Links Humans, Lemurs?" National Geographic News: *http://news.nationalgeographic.com/news/2009/05/090519-missing-link-found.html* (January 5, 2014).

[120] "Ida (Darwinius masillae): the Missing Link at Last? Does Ida Deserve the Attention? A Preliminary Comment," AnswersinGenesis.com: *http://www.answersingenesis.org/articles/2009/05/19/ida-missing-link* (January 5, 2014).

[121] Marvin L. Lubenow, "Recovery of Neandertal mDNA: An Evaluation," *CEN Technical Journal*, 12 (1) (1998): 89.

[122] Jack Cuozzo, "Buried Alive: The Truth about Neanderthal Man," *Truths That Transform Action Sheet* (Radio Program, aired on March 14–15, 2000).

[123] Lubenow, 1992, p. 63.

[124] DeWitt Steele & Gregory Parker, *Science of the Physical Creation*, 2nd ed (Pensacola, FL: A Beka Book, 1996), 301.

[125] M.L. Lubenow, "Recovery of Neandertal mDNA: An Evaluation," *CEN Technical Journal*, 12 (1) (1998): 89–90.

[126] Jack Cuozzo, *Buried Alive: The Startling Truth About Neanderthal Man* (Green Forest, AZ: Master Books, 1998), 162, 163, 203.

[127] Cuozzo, *Buried Alive: The Truth about Neanderthal Man* (2000).

[128] Green, R. E. et al. A Draft Sequence of the Neandertal Genome. *Science*. 328 (5979) (2010): 710–722.

[129] Steele & Parker, *Science of the Physical Creation*, pp. 301–302.

[130] Vance Ferrell, *The Evolution Cruncher* (Altamont, TN: Evolution Facts, Inc., 2001), 529.

[131] Lubenow, 1992, p. 235.

[132] Ian Taylor, "Fossil Man" Creation Moments Online: *http://www.creationmoments.com/content/fossil-man* (January 1, 2014).

[133] Vance Ferrell, *The Evolution Cruncher* (Altamont, TN: Evolution Facts, Inc., 2001), 529.

[134] Lubenow, 1992, p. 99.

[135] Eugene DuBois, "On the Fossil Human Skulls Recently Discovered in Java and Pithecanthropus Erectus," *Man*, 37 (January 1937): 4.

[136] Pat Shipman, "On the Trail of the Piltdown Fraudsters," *New Scientist*, 128 (October 6, 1990): 52.

[137] Lubenow, 1992, pp. 42–43.

[138] Lubenow, 1992, pp. 139–140.

[139] Richard Dawkins, *River out of Eden* (Basic Books, 1995), 98.

[140] John D. Morris, "Does 'The Beak of the Finch' Prove Darwin Was Right?" ICR.org: *http://www.icr.org/article/1135/* (January 1, 2014).

[141] This orchard model was developed by Dr. Kurt Wise and has been refined by many creation scientists over the years.

[142] Miller & Levine, *Biology,* pp. 466-467.

[143] Other translations, such as the NIV, translate this section as "great creatures of the sea." The Hebrew phrase used for "great sea creatures" is hattannînim haggədōlîm (־תאה מקנננאת מלדגגאה). The lemma gadôl (לְדאג) certainly means big or great great. Tannîn (נננאה) is often translated "sea monsters" or "dragons." Thus while the KJV translates this as "great whales," the term is broader. It would also include living large sea creatures like the great white shark and the whale shark. Surprising as it is to those used to faulty "millions of years" claims, the term would also include many famous extinct sea creatures. These include ichthyosaurs (from the Greek for "fish lizard"), somewhat like reptilian versions of dolphins; some grew huge, such as the 21-m (69-foot)–long Shastasaurus sikanniensis. Other creatures included in the term tannîn would be the short-necked long-headed pliosaurs, such as Liopleurodon, 6.4 (21 feet) long, although the 1999 BBC series Walking With Dinosaurs portrayed it as 25 m (82 ft.) long, far larger than any known specimen. There were also the long-necked plesiosaurs such as Elasmosaurus, 14 m (46 feet) long, half of it the neck. Other tannin created on Day 5 were mosasaurus, like marine versions of monitor lizards, the largest of which was Hainosaurus, at 17.5 meters (57 ft.) long.

[144] Werner, *Evolution: The Grand Experiment*, p. 40.

[145] N.D. Pyenson, et al., "Discovery of a Sensory Organ that Coordinates Lunge Feeding in Rorqual Whales," *Nature* 485 (7399) 2012: 498–501. J. Sarfati, "Baleen

Whales have Unique Sensory Organ," *Creation* 35 (4) (2013): 38–40.

[146] Charles Darwin, *The Origin of Species* 1st ed. (1865): Chapter 6, p. 184.

[147] Francis Darwin, *More Letters of Charles Darwin* (London: J. Murray, 1903): 162.

[148] Leigh Van Valen, "Deltatheridia, a New Order of Mammals," *Bulletin of the American Museum of Natural History* 132 (1966): 92.

[149] Philip D. Gingerich & D. E. Russell, "Pakicetus inachus, a new archaeocete (Mammalia, Cetacea) from the early-middle Eocene Kuldana Formation of Kohat (Pakistan)," *University of Michigan Museum of Paleontology*, 25 (1981): 235–246.

[150] University Of Michigan, "New Fossils Suggest Whales And Hippos Are Close Kin," *Science Daily* (September 20, 2001); University Of California, Berkeley, "UC Berkeley, French Scientists Find Missing Link Between The Whale And Its Closest Relative, The Hippo," *Science Daily* (February 7, 2005); Patricia Reaney, "Fossil Finds Show Whales Related to Early Pigs," Greenspun: *http://www.greenspun.com/bboard/q-and-a-fetch-msg.tcl?msg_id=006QvI.*

[151] Werner, *Evolution: The Grand Experiment*, p. 40.

[152] Casey Luskin, "Nice Try! A Review of Alan Rogers's The Evidence for Evolution," (October 18, 2011), Evolution News: *http://www.evolutionnews.org/2012/04/a_review_of_ala058641.html* (December 25, 2013).

[153] "Debate on Origins of Life," Discovery Institute: *http://www.discovery.org/v/1711*, (December 25, 2013).

[154] Luskin, 2011.

[155] Miller & Levine, *Biology*, p. 466.

[156] Philip D. Gingerich, NA. Wells, Donald Russell, S.M. Shaw, "Origin of Whales in Epicontinental Remnant

Seas: New Evidence from the Early Eocene of Pakistan," *Science* 220 (4595) (April 22, 1983): 403–406.

[157] Phillip Gingerich, "The Whales of Tethys," *Natural History*, (April 1994): 86.

[158] P.D. Gingerich, "Evidence for Evolution from the Vertebrate Fossil Record," *Journal for Geological Education*, 31 (1983): 140-144.

[159] Christian de Muizon, "Walking with Whales," *Nature* 413, (September 20, 2001): 259–260.

[160] G.M. Thewissen, E.M. Williams, L.J. Roe, & S.T. Hussain, "Skeletons of Terrestrial Cetaceans and the Relationship of Whales to Artiodactyls," *Nature* 413 (September, 2001): 277-281.

[161] David Quammen, "Was Darwin Wrong?" *National Geographic*, 206 (5) (November, 2004): 2–35.

[162] Fossilworks Paleobiology Database: *http://fossilworks.org* (December 25, 2013).

[163] Miller & Levine, *Biology*, p. 466.

[164] Michael Denton, *Evolution: A Theory in Crisis*, (Bethesda: Adler & Adler, 1985), 210-211,

[165] Werner, *Evolution: The Grand Experiment*, pp. 137–138.

[166] Fossilworks Paleobiology Database: *http://fossilworks.org* (December 25, 2013).

[167] J. G. M. Thewissen & E. M. Williams, "The Early Radiations of Cetacea (Mammalia): Evolutionary Pattern and Developmental Correlations," *Annual Review of Ecological Systems*, 33 (2002): 73–90.

[168] Miller & Levine, *Biology*, p. 466.

[169] Working Group on Teaching Evolution, "National Academy of Sciences Teaching about Evolution and the Nature of Science, (Washington, D.C.: National Academy Press, 1998): 18.

[170] Carl Werner, *Evolution: The Grand Experiment* (DVD) (Based on interview conducted on August 28, 2001),

(Green Forest, AR: New Leaf Publishing Group/Audio Visual Consultants Inc.).

171 "Basilosaurus," Celebrating 100 Years: Explore Our Collections, Smithsonian National Museum of Natural History: *http://www.mnh.si.edu* (February 10, 2012).

172 Phillip Gingerich, *The Press-Enterprise*, (July 1, 1990): A-15.

173 Philip Gingerich, B. Holly Smith, & Elwyn L. Simons, "Hind limbs of Eocene Basilosaurus: Evidence of Feet in Whales," Science, Vol. 249, (July 13, 1990): 156.

174 "Whales with 'non–feet,'" Creation.com: *http://creation.com/focus-142#nonfeet* (December 26, 2013).

175 Jonathan Sarfati, "Science, Creation and Evolutionism: Response to the Latest Anticreationist Agitprop from the US National Academy of Sciences (NAS)," Creation.com: *http://creation.com/science-creation-and-evolutionism-refutation-of-nas* (December 26, 2013).

176 D.T. Gish, *Evolution: The Fossils still say no!* (El Cajon, CA: Institute for Creation Research, 1985): 206–208.

177 Jonathan Silvertown (ed), *99% Ape: How Evolution Adds Up* (University of Chicago Press, 2009), 4.

178 Various sources will show minor differences in these comparisons. They are for example only.

179 Silvertown, 2009.

180 PBS NOVA, "Darwins' Predictions," PBS: *http://www.pbs.org/wgbh/nova/id/pred-nf.html* (December 11, 2013).

181 This comes from comparing the total base pairs to the "golden path length" in the Ensemble database (*http://useast.ensembl.org/Homo_sapiens/Info/StatsTable?db=core* (January 1, 2014). These numbers should be the same. As long as they are different, there is uncertainty in the number of base pairs in the genome.

182 Jeffery P. Demuth, Tijl De Bie, Jason E. Stajich, Nello Cristianini, & Matthew W. Hahn, "The Evolution of Mammalian Gene Families," *PLOS ONE*, 10 (2006).

[183] Richard Buggs, "Chimpanzee?" RD.NL: *http://www.refdag.nl/chimpanzee_1_282611* (December 11, 2013).

[184] Jeffrey P. Tomkins, "Comprehensive Analysis of Chimpanzee and Human Chromosomes Reveals Average DNA Similarity of 70%," *Answers Research Journal* 6 (2013): 63–69.

[185] Mary-Claire King & A. C. Wilson, "Evolution at Two Levels in Humans and Chimpanzees," *Science* 188 (1975): 107–116.

[186] R.J Rummel, "Statistics of Democide: Genocide and Mass Murder Since 1900," *School of Law, University of Virginia* (1997); and Transaction Publishers, Rutgers University (2013).

[187] J. Bergman & J. Tomkins, "Is the Human Genome Nearly Identical to Chimpanzee? A Reassessment of the Literature." *Journal of Creation* 26 (2012): 54–60.

[188] Bergman & Tomkins, 2012.

[189] J. Tomkins, "How Genomes are Sequenced and why it Matters: Implications for Studies in Comparative Genomics of Humans and Chimpanzees," *Answers Research Journal* 4 (2011): 81–88.

[190] I. Ebersberger, D. Metzler, C. Schwarz, & S. Pääbo, "Genomewide Comparison of DNA Sequences between Humans and Chimpanzees," *American Journal of Human Genetics* 70 (2002): 1490–1497.

[191] Chimpanzee Sequencing and Analysis Consortium, "Initial Sequence of the Chimpanzee Genome and Comparison with the Human Genome," *Nature* 437 (2005): 69–87.

[192] J. Tomkins, "Genome-Wide DNA Alignment Similarity (Identity) for 40,000 Chimpanzee DNA Sequences Queried against the Human Genome is 86–89%," *Answers Research Journal* 4 (2011): 233–241.

[193] J. Prado-Martinez, et al. "Great Ape Genetic Diversity and Population History," *Nature* 499 (2013), 471–475.

194 J. Tomkins, & J. Bergman. "Genomic Monkey Business—Estimates of Nearly Identical Human-Chimp DNA Similarity Re-evaluated using Omitted Data," *Journal of Creation* 26 (2012), 94–100; J. Tomkins, "Comprehensive Analysis of Chimpanzee and Human Chromosomes Reveals Average DNA Similarity of 70%," *Answers Research Journal* 6 (2013): 63–69.

195 Tomkins & Bergman, 2013.

196 Tomkins, 2011.

197 Tomkins, 2013.

198 Tomkins, 2011.

199 E. Wijaya, M.C. Frith, P. Horton & K. Asai, "Finding Protein-coding Genes through Human Polymorphisms," *PloS one* 8 (2013).

200 M. J. Hangauer, I.W. Vaughn & M. T. McManus, "Pervasive Transcription of the Human Genome Produces Thousands of Previously Unidentified Long Intergenic Noncoding RNAs," *PLoS genetics* 9 (2013).

201 S. Djebali, et al. "Landscape of Transcription in Human Cells," *Nature* 489 (2012): 101–108.

202 M. D. Paraskevopoulou, et al. "DIANA-LncBase: Experimentally Verified and Computationally Predicted MicroRNA Targets on Long Non-coding RNAs," *Nucleic Acids Research* 41 (2013): 239–245.

203 G. Liu, J.S. Mattick, & R. J. Taft, "A Meta-analysis of the Genomic and Transcriptomic Composition of Complex Life," *Cell Cycle* 12 (2013), 2061–2072.

204 J. J Yunis & O. Prakash, "The Origin of Man: A Chromosomal Pictorial Legacy," *Science* 215 (1982): 1525–1530.

205 J. W. Ijdo, A. Baldini, D.C. Ward, S. T. Reeders & R. A. Wells, "Origin of Human Chromosome 2: An Ancestral Telomere-telomere Fusion," *Proceedings of the National Academy of Sciences of the United States of America* 88 (1991): 9051–9055.

[206] J. Bergman & J. Tomkins, "The Chromosome 2 Fusion Model of Human Evolution—Part 1: Re-evaluating the Evidence," *Journal of Creation* 25 (2011): 110–114.

[207] J. Tomkins, "Alleged Human Chromosome 2 'Fusion Site' Encodes an Active DNA Binding Domain Inside a Complex and Highly Expressed Gene—Negating Fusion," *Answers Research Journal* 6 (2013): 367–375.

[208] Y. Fan, E. Linardopoulou, C. Friedman, E. Williams & B.J. Trask, "Genomic Structure and Evolution of the Ancestral Chromosome Fusion Site in 2q13-2q14.1 and Paralogous Regions on other Human Chromosomes," *Genome Research* 12 (2002): 1651–1662; Y. Fan, T. Newman, E. Linardopoulou, & B.J. Trask, "Gene Content and Function of the Ancestral Chromosome Fusion Site in Human Chromosome 2q13-2q14.1 and Paralogous Regions," *Genome Research* 12 (2002): 1663–1672.

[209] Y.Z. Wen, L. L. Zheng, L.H. Qu, F. J. Ayala & Z.R. Lun, Z. R, "Pseudogenes are not Pseudo Any More," *RNA Biology* 9 (2012): 27–32.

[210] J. Tomkins, "The Human Beta-Globin Pseudogene Is Non-Variable and Functional," *Answers Research Journal* 6 (2013): 293–301.

[211] M. Y. Lachapelle, & G. Drouin, "Inactivation Dates of the Human and Guinea Pig Vitamin C Genes," *Genetica* 139 (2011): 199–207.

[212] J. Sanford, *Genetic Entropy and the Mystery of the Genome,* 3rd ed. (FMS Publications, 2010).

[213] J. Tomkins & J. Bergman, "Incomplete Lineage Sorting and Other 'Rogue' Data Fell the Tree of Life," *Journal of Creation* 27 (2013): 63–71.

[214] P. Senter, "Vestigial Skeletal Structures in Dinosaurs," *Journal of Zoology,* 280 (1) (January 2010): 60–71.

[215] Thomas Heinze, *Creation vs. Evolution Handbook* (Grand Rapids, MI: Baker, 1973).

[216] Isaac Asimov, *1959 Words of Science* (New York: Signet Reference Books, 1959), 30.

[217] J. Bergman, "Are Wisdom Teeth (third molars) Vestiges of Human Evolution?" *CEN Tech Journal*. 12 (3) (1998): 297–304.

[218] Charles Darwin, *The Descent of Man and Selection in Relation to Sex* (London: John Murray, 1871), 21.

[219] Charles Darwin, *The Origin of Species* (New York: Modern Library, 1859), 346–350.

[220] S. R. Scadding, "Do Vestigial Organs Provide Evidence for Evolution?" *Evolutionary Theory* 5 (1981): 173–176.

[221] Robert Wiedersheim, *The Structure of Man: An Index to his Past History* (London: Macmillan, 1895, Translated by H. and M. Bernard).

[222] David Starr Jordan & Vernon Lyman Kellogg, *Evolution and Animal Life* (New York: Appleton, 1908), 175.

[223] Wiedersheim, 1895, p. 3.

[224] Darwin, 1871, p. 29.

[225] Cora A. Reno, *Evolution on Trial* (Chicago: Moody Press, 1970), 81.

[226] Diane Newman, *The Urinary Incontinence Sourcebook* (Los Angeles, CA.: Lowell House, 1997), 13.

[227] Warren Walker, *Functional Anatomy of the Vertebrates: An Evolutionary Perspective* (Philadelphia, PA: Saunders, 1987), 253.

[228] Catherine Parker Anthony, *Textbook of Anatomy and Physiology*, 6th ed. (St. Louis, MO: Mosby, 1963), 411.

[229] Anthony Smith, *The Body* (New York: Viking Penguin, 1986), 134.

[230] Henry Gray, *Gray's Anatomy* (Philadelphia: Lea Febiger, 1966), 130.

[231] Dorothy Allford, *Instant Creation—Not Evolution* (New York: Stein and Day, 1978), 42; Saul Weischnitzer, *Outline of Human Anatomy* (Baltimore, MD: University Park Press, 1978), 285.

[232] J. D. Ratcliff, *Your Body and How it Works* (New York: Delacorte Press, 1975), 137.

[233] Lawrence Galton, "All those Tonsil Operations: Useless? Dangerous?" *Parade* (May 2, 1976): 26.

[234] Martin L. Gross, *The Doctors (*New York: Random House, 1966).

[235] Jacob Stanley, Clarice Francone, & Walter Lossow, *Structure and Function in Man,* 5th ed. (Philadelphia: Saunders, 1982).

[236] Alvin Eden, "When Should Tonsils and Adenoids be Removed?" *Family Weekly* (September 25, 1977): 24.

[237] Syzmanowski as quoted in Dolores Katz, "Tonsillectomy: Boom or Boondoggle?" *The Detroit Free Press (*April 13, 1966).

[238] Katz, 1972, p. 1-C.

[239] N. J. Vianna, Petter Greenwald & U. N. Davies, "Tonsillectomy" In: *Medical World News* (September 10, 1973).

[240] Katz, 1972.

[241] Darwin, 1871, pp. 27–28.

[242] Peter Raven & George Johnson, *Understanding Biology* (St. Louis: Times Mirror Mosby, 1988), 322.

[243] Rebecca E. Fisher, "The Primate Appendix: A Reassessment," *The Anatomical Record*, 261 (2000): 228–236.

[244] R. Randal Bollinger, Andrew S. Barbas, Errol L. Bush, Shu S. Lin and William Parker, "Biofilms in the Large Bowel Suggest an Apparent Function of the Human Vermiform Appendix," *Journal of Theoretical Biology*, 249 (4) (2007): 826–831; Thomas Morrison (ed.). *Human Physiology* (New York: Holt, Rinehart, and Winston, 1967).

[245] Loren Martin, "What is the Function of the Human Appendix?" *Scientific American Online* (1999).

[246] Thomas Judge & Gary R. Lichtenstein, "Is the Appendix a Vestigial Organ? Its Role in Ulcerative Colitis," *Gastroenterology*, 121 (3) (2001): 730–732.

[247] Rod R. Seeley, Trent D. Stephens, & Philip Tate, *Anatomy and Physiology* (Boston: McGraw-Hill, 2003).

[248] Ernst Haeckel, *The Evolution of Man: A Popular Exposition of the Principal Points of Human Ontogeny and Phylogeny* (New York: D. Appleton, 1879), 438.

[249] Wiedersheim, 1895, p. 163.

[250] O. Levy, G. Dai, C. Riedel, C.S. Ginter, E.M. Paul, A. N. Lebowitz & N. Carrasco, "Characterization of the thyroid Na+/I- symporter with an anti-COOH terminus antibody," *Proceedings from the National Academy of Science*, 94 (1997): 5568–5573.

[251] Albert Maisel, "The useless glands that guard our health." *Reader's Digest* (November, 1966): 229–235.

[252] John Clayton, "Vestigial Organs Continue to Diminish," *Focus on Truth*, 6 (6) (1983): 6–7.

[253] Seeley, Stephens, & Tate, *Anatomy and Physiology* (McGraw-Hill Education, 2003), 778.

[254] Maisel, 1966, p. 229.

[255] Arthur Guyton, *Textbook of Medical Physiology* (Philadelphia: W. B. Saunders, 1966): 139.

[256] Helen G. Durkin & Byron H. Waksman. "Thymus and Tolerance. Is Regulation the Major Function of the Thymus?" *Immunological Reviews*, 182 (2001): 33–57.

[257] Durkin & Waksman, 2001, p. 49.

[258] Benedict Seddon & Don Mason, "The Third Function of the Thymus," *Immunology Today*, 21 (2) (2000): 95–99.

[259] Maisel, 1966.

[260] Joel R. L. Ehrenkranz, "A Gland for all Seasons," *Natural History*, 92 (6) (1983): 18.

[261] Stanley Yolles, "The Pineal Gland," *Today's Health*, 44 (3) (1966): 76–79.

[262] David Blask, "Potential Role of the Pineal Gland in the Human Menstrual Cycle," Chapter 9 in *Changing Perspectives on Menopause,* Edited by A. M. Voda (Austin: University of Texas Press, 1982), 124.

[263] A. C. Greiner & S. C. Chan, "Melatonin Content of the Human Pineal Gland," *Science*, 199 (1978): 83–84.

[264] Esther Greisheimer & Mary Wideman, *Physiology and Anatomy*, 9th ed. (Philadelphia: Lippincott, 1972).

[265] Rosa M. Sainz, Juan C. Mayo, R.J. Reiter, D.X. Tan, and C. Rodriguez, "Apoptosis in Primary Lymphoid Organs with Aging," *Microscopy Research and Technique*, 62 (2003): 524–539.

[266] Sharon Begley & William Cook, "The SAD Days of Winter," *Newsweek*, 155 (2) (January 14, 1985): 64.

[267] Sainz, et al., 2003.

[268] G.J. Maestroni, A. Conti, & P. Lisson, "Colony-stimulating activity and hematopoietic rescue from cancer chemotherapy compounds are induced by melatonin via endogenous interleukin," *Cancer Research*, 54 (1994): 4740-4743.

[269] B.D. Jankovic, K. Isakovic, S. Petrovic, "Effect of Pinealectomy on Immune Reactions in the Rat," *Immunology*, 18 (1) (1970): 1–6.

[270] Lennert Wetterberg, Edward Geller, & Arthur Yuwiler, "Harderian Gland: An Extraretinal Photoreceptor Influencing the Pineal Gland in Neonatal Rats?" *Science*, 167 (1970): 884–885.

[271] Ehrenkranz, 1983, p. 18.

[272] Philip Stibbe, "A Comparative Study of the Nictitating Membrane of Birds and Mammals," *Journal of Anatomy,* 163 (1928): 159–176.

[273] Darwin, 1871, p. 23.

[274] Henry Drummond, *The Ascent of Man* (New York: James Potts and Co., 1903).

[275] Richard Snell & Michael Lemp, *Clinical Anatomy of the Eye* (Boston: Blackwell Scientific Pub, 1997), 93.

[276] Eugene Wolff (Revised by Robert Warwick), *Anatomy of the Eye and Orbit* 7th ed. (Philadelphia: W B. Saunders, 1976), 221.

[277] John King, Personal communication, Dr. King is a professor of ophthalmology at The Ohio State School of Medicine and an authority on the eye (October 18, 1979).

[278] E. P. Stibbe, "A Comparative Study of the Nictitating Membrane of Birds and Mammals," *Journal of Anatomy* 62 (1928): 159–176.

[279] Wiedersheim, 1895.

[280] D. Peck, "A Proposed Mechanoreceptor Role for the Small Redundant Muscles which Act in Parallel with Large Prime movers" in P. Hinick, T. Soukup, R. Vejsada, & J. Zelena's (eds.) *Mechanoreceptors: Development, Structure and Function* (New York: Plenum Press, 1988), 377–382.

[281] David N. Menton, "The Plantaris and the Question of Vestigial Muscles in Man," *CEN Technical Journal*, 14 (2) (2000): 50–53.

[282] Herbert DeVries, *Physiology of Exercise for Physical Education and Athletics* (Dubuque, IA: William C. Brown, 1980), 16–18.